AN INTRODUCTION TO
COMPONENT-BASED
SOFTWARE DEVELOPMENT

SERIES ON COMPONENT-BASED SOFTWARE DEVELOPMENT

Aims and Scope

In Software Engineering, component-based development (CBD) is concerned with constructing systems from pre-built software units, or components. A system is developed not as a monolithic entity, but as a composite of sub-parts that have already been built separately, possibly by third parties (and deposited in a repository). There are many different views on exactly what components are and how they are composed, but there is universal agreement on the cost benefits of CBD: reduced development cost and time (via reuse), and hence reduced time-to-market. There are also differing opinions on whether CBD, first proposed in the Sixties, is still relevant today. Our view is that with software becoming ever more pervasive societally, large-scale and complex, CBD can only become more, not less, relevant. The software challenges posed by the relentless march towards a smart inter-connected world: the Internet of Things, self-driving cars, etc., demand ever increasing scalability, complexity, and above all safety. We believe that with more research and development, these are precisely the other benefits that CBD, in particular compositionality, will be able to bring in future, by means of hierarchical construction and compositional V&V.

The aim of this series is to publish both teaching and research material on all aspects of CBD: from course text books to research monographs.

Call for Contributions

If you have suitable ideas or material for the series, please contact the Editor-in-Chief:

Kung-Kiu Lau
School of Computer Science
The University of Manchester
Manchester M13 9PL
United Kingdom
kung-kiu.lau@manchester.ac.uk

Series on Component-Based Software Development – Vol. 3

AN INTRODUCTION TO COMPONENT-BASED SOFTWARE DEVELOPMENT

KUNG-KIU LAU
SIMONE DI COLA
University of Manchester, UK

 **World Scientific**

NEW JERSEY · LONDON · SINGAPORE · BEIJING · SHANGHAI · HONG KONG · TAIPEI · CHENNAI · TOKYO

Published by

World Scientific Publishing Co. Pte. Ltd.

5 Toh Tuck Link, Singapore 596224

USA office: 27 Warren Street, Suite 401-402, Hackensack, NJ 07601

UK office: 57 Shelton Street, Covent Garden, London WC2H 9HE

Library of Congress Cataloging-in-Publication Data

Names: Lau, K.-K. (Kung-Kiu), 1953–   author. | Di Cola, Simone, author.

Title: An introduction to component-based software development / by Kung-Kiu Lau
(University of Manchester, UK), Simone di Cola (University of Manchester, UK).

Description: [Hackensack] New Jersey : World Scientific, 2017. | Series: Series on component-based
software development ; volume 3 | Includes bibliographical references and index.

Identifiers: LCCN 2017014303 | ISBN 9789813221871 (hc : alk. paper)

Subjects: LCSH: Component software.

Classification: LCC QA76.76.C66 L38 2017 | DDC 005.3--dc23

LC record available at https://lccn.loc.gov/2017014303

British Library Cataloguing-in-Publication Data

A catalogue record for this book is available from the British Library.

Desk Editor: Anthony Alexander

Typeset by Stallion Press
Email: enquiries@stallionpress.com

Printed in Singapore

Dedicated to our families, our colleagues, and our students

Preface

In terms of documentary evidence, Component-based Software Development can trace its origin to 1968. In a seminal paper, Doug McIlroy promulgated software components as mass produced software units that can be used repeatedly, i.e. reused, in a family of related software products, e.g. compilers for a language family. Indeed his idea was components for software product lines.

In the early days, software components were defined in different ways by different people. McIlroy described components variously as routines, modules, blackboxes, etc. Cox defined components as software integrated circuits. An attempt to unify the terminology only took place thirty years or so after McIlroy's 1968 paper. An international group of researchers conducted an extensive examination and discussion of the desiderata for software components. These desiderata now form the foundation of component-based software research.

A cornerstone of component-based software development is the notion of component models. A component model defines components as well as associated composition mechanisms. As such, it differentiates modern component-based software research from its earlier counterpart which focused predominantly on components only. With software becoming all pervasive and ever more complex and large-scale nowadays, it is increasingly obvious that composition holds the key to tackling not just scale and complexity in system construction but also safety. In the Internet of Things, including driverless cars, composition has a crucial role to play in ensuring tractability and above all safety.

This book provides an introductory account of the basic principles of component-based software development, and the various approaches that have emerged over the years. It is suitable as a student text book for an introductory course on component-based software development. It can also serve as an introduction to the research field in component-based software development.

The book is currently used for a Masters course at Manchester. We would like to thank all our students over the years for being — hopefully willing — guinea pigs but also for their feedback and suggestions for improvement.

As researchers, we have gathered and created some of the material of the book with many of our colleagues, both local and international, over the years. We would like to thank them all for their cooperation and contributions. We acknowledge our international collaborators in the appropriate chapters in the book. Here we would like to thank our colleagues at Manchester: Zheng Wang, Perla Velasco Elizondo, Ling Ling, Vladyslav Ukis, Cuong Tran, Faris Taweel, Yannis Ntalamagkas, Azlin Nordin, Petr Štěpán, Lily Safie, Keng-Yap Ng, Tauseef Rana, Rehman Arshad, Damian Arrelanes, Chen Qian and Nasser Al-Housni.

Kung-Kiu Lau and Simone Di Cola
March 2017, Manchester

About the Authors

Kung-Kiu Lau is currently a Senior Lecturer in the School of Computer Science at the University of Manchester, UK. He has been conducting research on Component-based Software Development for more than 10 years, with particular focus on component models that meet the requisite desiderata. He is the editor of a book series on Component-based Software Development, published by World Scientific, and a member of the editorial boards of the *Journal of Applied Logic* and the *Journal of Universal Computer Science*.

Simone di Cola is a Research Associate in the School of Computer Science at the University of Manchester, UK. He holds a PhD in Component-based Software Development from Manchester. His research has been on Component-based Modelling and Construction of Product Families using Enumerative Variability, and is the author of an industrial-strength tool for that purpose.

Contents

Chapter 1

Introduction

Component-based Software Development (CBD)[1] [Bachmann *et al.* (2000); (2001); Szyperski *et al.* (2002)] aims to compose systems from pre-built software units, or *components*. A system is developed not as a monolithic entity, but as a composite of sub-parts that have already been built separately. Such an approach reduces production cost by composing a system from pre-existing components, instead of building it from scratch. It also enables software reuse, since components can be reused in many systems. Thus CBD promises the benefits of: (i) reduced production cost; (ii) reduced time-to-market; and (iii) increased software reuse. These benefits have long been sought after by the software industry.

The basic idea of CBD is illustrated by Fig. 1.1: first, components are (designed and) built and deposited in a *repository*; then different systems can be (designed and) built by using components retrieved from the repository. By thus reusing repository components for multiple systems, we can reap the benefits of CBD.

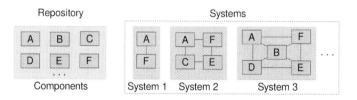

Fig. 1.1   Component-based software development.

The use of repository components for building systems suggests that CBD is essentially *bottom-up*, starting with pre-defined components, and composing them into a specific system; rather than *top-down*, starting with a top-level system

---

[1] Various abbreviations have been used, CBD and CBSE being the main ones. We choose CBD.

design, and successively decomposing it until components for this system are identified and then built just for this system.

In CBD, the life cycle of components [Christiansson *et al.* (2002)] consists of three stages: (i) the *design phase*, when components are designed, defined and constructed; (ii) the *deployment phase*, when components are deployed into the execution environment of the system under construction; and (iii) the *run-time* phase, when components are instantiated with data and executed in the running system.

Precisely what components are, and what desirable properties they should have in order to provide the requisite support for CBD, has been discussed at length [Broy *et al.* (1998); (2001); Szyperski *et al.* (2002); Meyer (2003)]. The resulting set of desiderata has been widely disseminated and accepted, and is summarised in the table in Fig. 1.2. The implications of these desiderata for the relevant phases of component life cycle (the design and deployment phases) are also included in this table.

Desideratum	Design Phase	Deployment Phase
Components should pre-exist	Deposit components in repository	Retrieve components from repository
Components should be produced independently	Use builder	—
Components should be deployed independently	—	Use assembler
It should be possible to copy and instantiate components	Copies possible	Copies and instances possible
It should be possible to build composites	Composition possible	Composition possible
It should be possible to store composites	Use repository	—

Fig. 1.2   Desiderata for component-based software development.

Firstly, for the purpose of system development, components should be pre-existing reusable software units, which system developers can reuse to compose software for different applications more quickly than writing all the code from scratch for each application. This necessitates the use of a *repository*, in which components can be deposited in the design phase of the component life cycle, and from which components can be retrieved in the deployment phase.

Secondly, components should be produced and used, or deployed, by independent parties. That is, component developers need not be the same people as component customers such as system developers. This is important for ensuring that components are truly reusable by third parties. It requires the use of tools that can interact with a repository: in the design phase, a *builder* tool is needed for building components and depositing them in the repository; in the deployment phase, an *assembler* tool is needed for assembling components (more accurately, component instances, see below) retrieved from the repository.

Thirdly, it should be possible to copy and instantiate components, so that their reuse can be maximised, both in terms of code reuse and in terms of components' scope of deployment. Thus, it should be possible to make distinct copies of components, and to distinguish components from their instances; and thus differentiate the design and deployment phases from the run-time phase of the component life cycle.

Fourthly, it should be possible to compose components into composite components, and then store these composite components. Composite components in turn can be composed with (composite) components into larger composites (or subsystems), and so on. This requires that, like their non-composite counterparts, composites can also be deposited in and retrieved from a repository. Composition means not only reuse, but also a systematic approach to system construction.

In addition to these desiderata, we have identified another ideal one: the possibility to perform composition in both design and deployment phases. Composition means component reuse, and therefore composition in both phases will maximise reuse. It also means design flexibility in the sense that the deployed components, in particular composite components, can be designed, by composition in either phase: either entirely in one phase or partially in both phases.

An idealised component life cycle should meet all the aforementioned desiderata, and we have defined such a life cycle [Lau and Wang (2005, 2007)].

1.1 An Idealised Component Life Cycle

Our idealised component life cycle is depicted in Fig. 1.3. It is derived from all the desiderata together with their life cycle implications listed in Fig. 1.2.

Figure 1.4 summarises the characteristics of the actors and artefacts involved in the idealised component life cycle.

1.1.1 *Design Phase*

In the design phase, components have to be constructed, catalogued and stored in a *repository* in such a way that they can be retrieved later, as and when needed. Components in the repository are in source code, or they may have been compiled into binary.

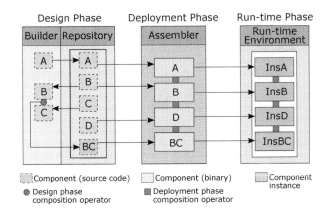

Fig. 1.3   An idealised component life cycle.

	Design Phase	Deployment Phase	Run-time Phase
Role	Component designer (producer/vendor)	System developer	System user
Environment	System independent	System specific	System execution environment
Component type	Template + deployment contracts	Deployed subsystem	Executable subsystem
Data in components	Place-holders	Place-holders + configuration data	All data initialised
Component format	Source or binary	Binary	Binary instance
Composition operators	Pre-defined	Pre-defined	——

Fig. 1.4   Characteristics of actors and artefacts in idealised component life cycle.

Components should be composed into well-defined *composites* using suitable *composition operators*, ideally supported by a composition theory. It should be also possible to store composites in, and retrieve them from the repository, and use them for further composition, like any components.

A *builder* tool can be used to (i) construct new components, and then deposit them in the repository, e.g. in Fig. 1.3, A is a new component constructed in the builder and deposited in the repository; (ii) retrieve components from the repository, compose them and deposit them back in the repository, e.g. in Fig. 1.3, B and C are retrieved from the repository and composed into a composite BC that is deposited in the repository.

To promote reuse, components in design phase should be *templates* that provide services. They should be identified and designed by domain experts as basic building blocks for the domain in question. They should be generic, rather than system-specific so that they could be (re)used to build many different applications. Similarly, composition operators in design phase should be generic composition schemes to coordinate components which can be customised for many different systems.

To support its reuse, any component should have an *interface*. In particular, a composite component should expose an interface generated during the composition process and its content should be determined according to the semantics of the composition operator involved.

Components in design phase should also include information of the environmental dependencies or resources needed for its deployment. Composition in design phase should generate such information for composites. For instance, deployment contracts [Lau and Ukis (2006)] could be used to specify this kind of information.

1.1.2 *Deployment Phase*

Ideally, composition in deployment-phase should follow on from, and thus exploit composition in design phase. That is, as far as possible, the composites here should be built directly from the (composite) components created in design phase.

In the deployment phase, components have to be retrieved from the repository, and if necessary compiled to *binary* code and then composed. The result of deployment phase composition is a whole *system* in binary code, and so this is the end result of system design and implementation. The completed system should be then *ready for execution*.

As in design-phase, composition should be carried out via *composition operators*. But in here, they should allow the coordination between components down to the last detail, as required by the specific application.

An *assembler* tool can be used to retrieve components from a repository, compile them into binary code, and then assemble them into a system. For example, in the assembler in Fig. 1.3, binaries of A, B, D and BC are retrieved and composed into a system.

Composite components in the deployment phase should have *interfaces* that allow them to be instantiated and executed at run-time phase. These interfaces should be generated during the composition process.

Composition in deployment-phase should be supported by suitable *deployment tools* to, for example, check the component compatibility with one another and with the execution environment, e.g. a tool for checking deployment contracts would be useful. Also with such tools, it should be possible to deploy a composite in many different systems.

1.1.3 *Run-time Phase*

In the run-time phase, the constructed system is *instantiated* and *executed* in the run-time environment, e.g. A, B, D and BC in the run-time environment in Fig. 1.3. Although this phase does not include further composition, for highly available applications it should be possible to perform some kind of adaptation on the component's *instances* in executable system.

1.2 Development Processes

The idealised component life cycle is about the stages of a component's life, starting from its creation and ending in its execution. These stages provide the basis of development processes for CBD. The desiderata of independent component production and deployment require that there is a separate development process for components, and hence a separate development process for systems built form components. We call these processes the *component life cycle* and the *system life cycle* respectively. As is standard practice in the literature, we will use 'life cycle' interchangeably with 'development process' or simply 'process'.

A number of development processes for CBD have been proposed, e.g. [Christiansson *et al.* (2002); Kotonya *et al.* (2003); Sommerville (2004a); Capretz (2005); Crnkovic *et al.* (2006)], to name but a few. (A survey can be found in [Kaur and Singh (2010)].) Naturally these processes all reflect the desiderata of CBD, and converge on the general view depicted in Fig. 1.5.

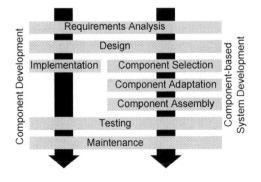

Fig. 1.5 CBD development processes.

The generic CBD process in Fig. 1.5 comprises two separate processes: (i) the *component life cycle*, for component development; (ii) the *system life cycle*, for component-based system development. Component development is also known as 'development *for* reuse', since it is concerned with developing components that can be stored in a repository and (re)used to build different systems. Component-based system development is also known as 'development *with* reuse', since it is concerned with developing systems by reusing pre-built components (the result of the component development process).

Each process follows the traditional Waterfall Model [Royce (1970); Benington (1983)] of 'requirements analysis, design, implementation, testing and maintenance'. For component development, implementation is a single activity, whereas for system development, implementation is a sequence of activities based on pre-built components, namely component selection, adaptation and assembly.

The component life cycle in Fig. 1.5 is not explicitly conformant with the idealised component life cycle as it does not explicitly specify independent component production or deployment, neither does it explicitly specify a repository of independently produced components. Moreover, it does not explicitly address V&V, i.e. Verification and Validation.

1.3 Verification and Validation

Verification is the process of evaluating the system under construction to check if it meets the specified requirements and design specifications. Complementary to verification, validation is the process of evaluating the system under construction to check if it meets the customer's requirements and expectations. Not surprisingly, testing plays a central role in V&V, e.g. system testing for verification, and acceptance testing for validation (see Fig. 1.6).

1.3.1 *The V Model*

For general (modular) system development, the standard model for V&V is the V Model [IABG (2017)], which is depicted in Fig. 1.6. The V Model is an adaptation of the traditional Waterfall Model for modular system development. It defines a sequential process consisting of phases for requirements, system specification, system or architectural design, module design, implementation and testing. Implementation consists of coding for the individual modules, and coding for integrating the modules into the entire system using the architectural design for the system. Testing follows coding. Thus the coding phase divides the whole process into 'development', the left arm of the V, and 'testing', the right arm of the V.

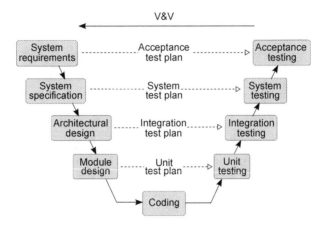

Fig. 1.6   The V Model.

During each of the development phases (in the left arm of the V), a test plan is drawn up for the corresponding testing activity (in the right arm of the V). For example, an acceptance test plan is drawn up from the requirements, since acceptance testing will be performed against the requirements. Similarly, unit test plans are generated from module design, since unit testing will be carried out on the modules, and so on.

Testing follows a sequential process, in reverse order of the development phases, as is usual for modular system development. Thus unit testing is performed first, followed by integration testing, system testing and finally acceptance testing. Each testing activity is carried out according to the test plan generated during the corresponding development phase.

The key property of the V Model that is pertinent here is that it is a *top-down* approach to system design and development, as Fig. 1.6 clearly shows. First, a top-level design is made of the architecture of the entire system; this identifies and specifies sub-systems or modules, and their inter-relationships. Then the individual modules are designed according to their specifications in the top-level design. In general, this top-down approach may be applied successively, each time decomposing sub-systems or modules in the current level of design into further sub-systems or modules. This decomposition is repeated as many times as is necessary, until a final design is arrived at in which the design of the system as well as all the individual modules is deemed complete, i.e. no further decomposition is necessary or desirable.

1.3.2 *Adapting the V Model for CBD*

Compared to the CBD processes in Fig. 1.5, which contain two life cycles, one for component development and one for system development, the V Model contains only one life cycle, for system development. So, the question is 'How can we adapt the V Model for V&V in CBD?'

The CBD processes in Fig. 1.5 shows CBD as an essentially *bottom-up* approach to system design, in the sense that components have to be developed first (in the component life cycle), and any particular system is constructed from these components (in the system life cycle). In contrast, as we have explained in the previous section, the V Model (Fig. 1.6) is essentially a *top-down* approach to system design: the system is designed first (thus identifying the requisite components), and then components are developed.

A straightforward adaptation of the V Model for CBD would be to retain the top-down approach to system design but use a component as a module, as shown in Fig. 1.7. For example, the V model adopted by the avionics industry as a CBD process (e.g. Airbus processes [da Cruz and Raistrick (2007); Gaufillet and Gabel (2010)]) is such an adaptation.

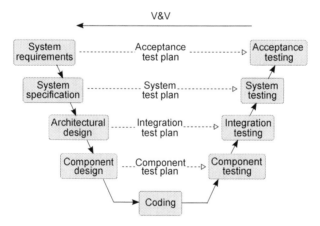

Fig. 1.7 Adapting the V Model for CBD.

However, such a straightforward adaptation of the V Model is at variance with the CBD processes in Fig. 1.5, precisely because it does not include a component life cycle and consequently does not incorporate the bottom-up nature of CBD.

An adaptation of the V Model for CBD that does incorporate the bottom-up nature of CBD is that of [Crnkovic *et al.* (2006)]. It does so by containing separate life cycles for component development and system development, like in Fig. 1.5.

However, this adaptation really applies the V Model only to its system life cycle; there is no evidence of the V Model in its component life cycle (which is the same as the one in Fig. 1.5).

In our view, to adapt the V Model properly for CBD, we need not only to incorporate both the component life cycle and the system life cycle, but also to apply the V Model to *both* of these cycles. We have defined such an adaptation, which we call the W Model,[2] for reasons that will become apparent later.

1.4   The W Model

The W Model is based on a bottom-up CBD process based on the idealised component life cycle (Section 1.1), as depicted in Fig. 1.8. This process consists of

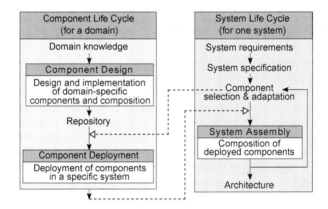

Fig. 1.8   A bottom-up CBD process based on the idealised component life cycle.

a component life cycle and a system life cycle, in line with the CBD processes in Fig. 1.5. However, it differs slightly from the latter, in that its component life cycle is the idealised component life cycle. In the design phase, components are (identified and) designed and constructed according to the domain requirements or knowledge [Lau and Taweel (2009)], and deposited into a *repository*. Components in the repository are domain-specific but not system-specific. In the deployment phase, components are retrieved from the repository and instantiated into executable component instances which are then deployed into a specific system under construction.

The system life cycle also differs slightly from that in Fig. 1.5 in that system design is now replaced by a completely bottom-up process of component *selection*

---

[2]The name W Model has been used by others, see Discussion and Further Reading.

(from the repository) and *adaptation*, followed by (component *deployment* in the component life cycle followed by) *system assembly*, which is simply the composition of the deployed components. The bottom-up nature of this process is indicated by an iterative loop in Fig. 1.8. It is worth noting that within this loop, the component life cycle links up with the system life cycle, since deployed components (from the component life cycle) are iteratively assembled into the system under construction (in the system life cycle). This link is denoted by the arrows between the two life cycles in Fig. 1.8, via the step of component selection and adaptation, and the step of component deployment.

Applying the V Model to both the component and system life cycles yields a CBD process with V&V as shown in Fig. 1.9. Compared to the straightforward

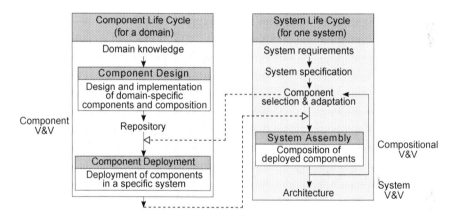

Fig. 1.9   A bottom-up CBD process with V&V.

adaptation of the V Model in Fig. 1.7, *component V&V* (which corresponds to component testing in Fig. 1.7) now occurs in the component life cycle, whilst *compositional V&V* (which corresponds to integration testing in Fig. 1.7) and *system V&V* (which corresponds to system testing in Fig. 1.7) occur in the system life cycle.

The bottom-up CBD process with V&V in Fig. 1.9 can be re-cast straightforwardly as a process with two conjoined V Models, one for the component life cycle and one for the system lifecycle. These two V Models are conjoined via the step of component selection, adaptation, and deployment. This 'double V' process is shown in Fig. 1.10. We call it the W Model.[3]

---

[3] In English, W is 'double u'; there is no letter for 'double v'.

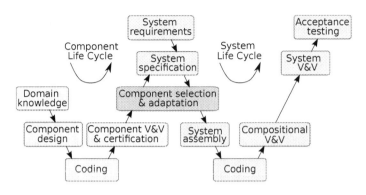

Fig. 1.10   The W Model.

Discussion and Further Reading

Much of the CBD literature originates from the International Symposium on Component-based Software Engineering (http://cbse-conferences. org/). A survey of the research published at this conference can be found in [Maras *et al.* (2012)].

The W Model

In the definition of the W Model, we need to specify a component model (Chapter 4) that defines the components and their composition accordingly. We have used a component model called X-MAN that we have defined ourselves. The details of X-MAN can be found in Section 7.1.

The name W Model has been used in software testing [Spillner (2002)] and product line engineering [Li *et al.* (2008)] in the context of traditional (i.e. non-CBD) software engineering. [Spillner (2002)] extends the V Model by adding a branch that integrates testing with debugging and code changes. [Li *et al.* (2008)] applies the V Model to domain engineering and application engineering in software product lines. This is similar to our approach, except that they do not use components and component composition, or the idealised component life cycle.

In the context of CBD, our W Model is similar to standard CBD processes, e.g. [Christiansson *et al.* (2002); Kotonya *et al.* (2003); Sommerville (2004a); Crnkovic *et al.* (2006)], in that they both contain separate life cycles for components and systems. However, unlike these processes, its component life cycle is the idealised one, which meets all the CBD desiderata in the literature [Broy *et al.* (1998)]. In particular the idealised component life cycle defines component composition in both component design and component deployment phases.

This emphasis on composition results in compositionality, which is an important property that is beneficial for practical system development, since it enables hierarchical system development and compositional reasoning.

The component life cycle of our W Model is similar to that in the Y Model [Capretz (2005)], in that they are both based on ideas stemming out from domain engineering. In the Y Model, components are developed using domain engineering techniques, and then archived. A framework is then defined for selecting components from the archive, and for assembling them into systems. The archive is of course just a repository. The framework is a structure for assembling components. Therefore, it is like a system assembler. However, the Y Model does not apply the V Model in any way to its component life cycle.[4] Moreover, it does not define a component model.

Other proposed processes for CBD, found in [Kotonya *et al.* (2003)], lack the separate process of deriving and developing components. Components are identified along with system development or received from some component space. Such component identification is not systematic and potentially leads to ad hoc components with limited reuse. Also, only [Kotonya *et al.* (2003)] suggests verification for components (in a system) and systems.

Other software development approaches based on domain engineering, e.g. product lines [Clements and Northrop (2015); Pohl *et al.* (2005)] and generative programming [Czarnecki and Eisenecker (2000)], are similar to the Y Model, in that they also do not apply the V Model to their component life cycle. Thus despite their use of domain engineering techniques for developing components, all these approaches do not follow a development process like the W Model.

On the other hand, the W Model is applicable to the V&V of product lines and generative programs. Unlike component models based on architecture description languages (see Chapter 6, the X-MAN component model, that underlies the W Model, defines explicit composition connectors. In the component life cycle of the W Model, along with components, composition connectors can be identified from domain requirements. These domain-specific components and composition connectors effectively define a domain-specific component model [Lau and Taweel (2009)]. In general, for a given domain, a domain-specific component model is the best one to use [Medvidovic *et al.* (2007)]. Furthermore, in a domain-specific component model, composition connectors can define product lines. Thus X-MAN can offer a component-based definition of product lines and generative programming.

---

[4]The same is true of component models that incorporate domain engineering techniques, e.g. EAST-ADL (2016).

In most of the related work, the process of identifying and constructing components (if exists) does not necessarily produce components in the component repository. Components can be developed by external parties and end up in some component pool or library. More importantly, components are not suggested to be derived from domain engineering of a domain. Therefore, components are not domain specific components. That leads to a major issue in that components in the pool are not suitable for a new application in the domain. In order to be reused, components are then required to be adapted or glue code is needed to wire up components. Even so, it is not feasible every time. In contrast, in our approach, components and connectors are derived from domain analysis. Components and connectors in a domain can be exhaustively identified including all possible variations. Moreover, components in repository are fully implemented and verified. Hence, the above issue does not arise.

For the purpose of V&V, our W Model is different from other adaptations of CBD processes based on the V Model for modular system design. The W Model contains a V model for both component and system life cycles, whereas other adaptations, e.g. [Crnkovic *et al.* (2006)], contain only a V model for the system life cycle. The value of a V Model for the component life cycle is that we can do component V&V and store pre-verified components in the repository. These components could be certified according to certain standards. Then, compositional V&V of composites can be carried out by re-using component V&V.

Chapter 2

What are Software Components?

What exactly are software components? This question is clearly fundamental to CBD and has been discussed thoroughly (see e.g. [Broy *et al.* (1998)]). The most widely adopted definition of a software component is the following by Szyperski [Szyperski *et al.* (2002)]:

> "A software component is a *unit of composition* with contractually specified *interfaces* and explicit *context dependencies* only. A software component can be deployed independently and is subject to composition by third parties."

This defines a software component as a unit of composition, with an interface; this definition has been universally accepted. Independent composition and deployment (by third parties) is in line with the idealised component life cycle (as discussed in Section 1.1). However, Szyperski's definition does not say anything about composition or context dependencies, in particular how they are defined.

Another component definition is due to Meyer [Meyer (2003)]:

> "A component is a software element (modular unit) satisfying the following conditions:
> 1. It can be used by other software elements, its 'clients'.
> 2. It possesses an official usage description, which is sufficient for a client author to use it.
> 3. It is not tied to any fixed set of clients."

Here, the notion of a component as a modular unit that can be used by other modular units harks back to the pre-CBD days of modular software development. In those days, composition was predominantly viewed as linking software units that are parametrised structures such as modules (see Chapter 3), and units were combined via usage links and parameters, the latter constituting their interfaces. In contrast, in CBD composition is not limited to linking modules (again see Chapter 3), since there are other kinds of components than modules.

Meyer's definition does not explicitly mention component interfaces. Instead it stipulates an official page of usage description for a component, which could serve as its 'interface'. As for the idealised component life cycle, it is not clear how well this definition aligns with it, since clients here are software elements (not third-party developers), referred to here as 'client authors'.

Yet another component definition is the following by Heineman and Councill (2001):

> "A [component is a] software element that conforms to a component model and can be independently deployed and composed without modification according to a composition standard."

This definition relies on a *component model* to define both components and composition. However, it does not say explicitly what a component model is, but only hints that it includes a composition standard.

The definition by Heineman and Councill offers the fullest scope for defining components and composition properly. So we believe components and composition should be defined in the context of a component model, and we have defined component models as follows [Lau and Wang (2007)]:

> A *software component model* is a definition of:
>
> - the *semantics* of components, i.e. what components are meant to be;
> - the *syntax* of components, i.e. how they are defined, constructed and represented;
> - the *composition* of components, i.e. how they are composed or assembled.

We will discuss component models in Chapter 4.

2.1 Generic Software Components

Apart from the aforementioned component definitions, there are many others. From all these definitions, a generally accepted view of a software component has emerged: it is a software unit with *provided services* and *required services*

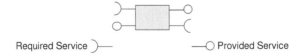

Fig. 2.1   A generic software component.

(Fig. 2.1). The provided services (represented by lollipops) are operations performed by the component. The required services (represented by sockets) are the services needed by the component to produce the provided services. Roughly speaking, the provided services of a component are its output, while the required services are its input. Required services are typically input values for parameters of the provided services.

The provided and required services of a component constitute its *interface*. The interface is the only point of access to the component; therefore it should provide all the information that is necessary to use the component. It should give the specifications of its provided and required services. It should also specify any *dependencies* between its provided and required services. To specify these dependencies precisely, it is necessary to match the required services to the corresponding provided ones. This matching could be expressed by listing corresponding services as ordered pairs $\langle r_1, p_1 \rangle, \ldots, \langle r_n, p_n \rangle$, where each r_i and p_i is a set of services.

Note that according to some definitions in the literature, a component can have multiple interfaces, with each interface as a different set of services. Here we have used a single interface as a collective entity for all such interfaces.

Generic components can be composed via their services. A provided service can be 'composed' with a matching required service, and vice versa. Precisely how services are 'composed' depends on how services are defined. The interface of a composite component, and hence a system, can be derived from the services of the sub-components. Again, precisely how this interface is derived depends on how component composition is defined in terms of service 'composition'.

With generic components and their composition defined above, the basic idea for CBD (Fig. 1.1) can be depicted as in Fig. 2.2. Composites, and eventually

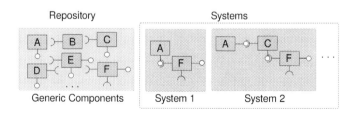

Fig. 2.2   Component-based software development with generic components.

complete systems, are composed from repository components, and successively from the resulting intermediate composites.

An example of a system built form generic components is the ATM system in Fig. 2.3. In this system, the *ATM* component provides the customers with a card reader and a keypad to enter their PINs and make requests such as 'withdraw'

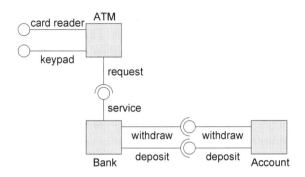

Fig. 2.3   ATM system using generic components.

and 'deposit', and passes the customer request on to the *Bank* component. The bank component provides the service (withdraw or deposit) that the customer has requested, by passing these requests on to the *Account* component, which provides these services.

2.2   Types of Components in Current Practice

There are three main types of components that are currently used in practice: (i) *objects* (Fig. 2.4(a)), as in object-oriented programming; (ii) *architectural units* (Fig. 2.4(b)), as in software architectures [Shaw and Garlan (1996); Bass *et al.* (2012)]; and (iii) *encapsulated components* (Fig. 2.4(c)), as in components with no external dependencies.

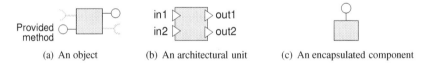

(a) An object   (b) An architectural unit   (c) An encapsulated component

Fig. 2.4   The three main types of components that are currently used in practice.

Each of these types is a variation of the generic component. An object's methods are its provided services, but an object has no visible required services (hence the blurring out in Fig. 2.4(a)). An architectural unit has input ports as required services, and output ports as provided services. An encapsulated component has only provided services but no required ones.

Objects as components will be discussed in Chapter 5, architectural units as components in Chapter 6, and encapsulated components in Chapter 7.

Discussion and Further Reading

Doug McIlroy [McIlroy (1968)] is credited with introducing the notion of software components. In fact he promulgated mass produced software components, even product lines (or families of related products). He considered components to be routines (or procedures) that can be used together in building a system. He also described components as modules, interchangeable parts and black boxes.

In [Cox (1986)], Cox defined software integrated circuits as components in object-oriented software development. These software units with pins or plugs as in silicon chips are of course a form of architectural units.

An extensive discussion about what components are, or should be, can be found in [Broy *et al.* (1998)], which lists definitions offered by many contributors. Definitions include: 'a group of related classes', 'data capsule', 'binary unit', 'self-contained entity'. The discussion in this book provides the widely accepted desiderata for CBD that underpin the idealised component life cycle (see Section 1.1).

Chapter 3

What is Software Composition?

Composition is of fundamental importance in CBD: it is indeed its essence. A component is a unit of composition, and therefore the meaning of a component depends on the meaning of composition. More specifically, components are composed by their services; therefore what these services are and how they are composed lie at the heart of CBD.

Before discussing component composition in particular, it is informative to first consider software composition in general.

Software composition [Nierstrasz and Meijler (1995)] refers to the composition of software constructs into larger composite constructs. The primary motivation for software composition is reuse [Sametinger (1997)], but composition also provides a means for systematic software construction. Of course, both software reuse and systematic software construction are also fundamental objectives for CBD.

In the most general terms, composition can be defined as any possible and meaningful interaction between the software constructs involved. A composition mechanism defines such an interaction. Clearly there are many different possible kinds of software constructs, with corresponding composition mechanisms [Bracha and Cook (1990); Nierstrasz and Tsichritzis (1995); Shaw and Garlan (1996); Sametinger (1997); Kiczales et al. (1997); Szyperski (2002b); Szyperski et al. (2002); Alonso et al. (2004); Ducasse et al. (2006); Aßmann (2003); Prehofer (2002); Ossher et al. (1996)]. Simple type definitions can be composed into compound types by type composition [Buchi and Weck (1998)]; arbitrary chunks of code can be joined together with glue and scripts [Schneider and Nierstrasz (1999)]; typed constructs can be linked by message passing, e.g. direct method calls between objects, or port connections between architectural units [Shaw and Garlan (1996); Bass et al. (2012)]; and so on.

In CBD it is desirable to have software constructs that make good composition units [Pfister and Szyperski (1996)], together with suitable composition mechanisms that facilitate both reuse and systematic construction [Achermann and Nierstrasz (2005)]. In addition, CBD also seeks to automate composition as much as possible, so as to provide good tool support and to reduce time-to-market as well.

3.1   Different Views of Software Composition

There are different views of software composition in the literature, that is various perceptions (and definitions) of what composition means in all the relevant software communities. In all these views, the baseline is that composition is performed on software entities that are perceived as meaningful *units of composition*. We will focus on units of composition that define *behaviour*, rather than constructs that define primitive types or pure data structures. Composition mechanisms compose units of composition into larger pieces of software, i.e. they compose pieces of behaviour into larger pieces of behaviour.

In this section, we outline the different views of composition and briefly discuss the generic nature of the associated units of composition and composition mechanisms.

3.1.1   *The Programming View*

One view of software composition is that it is simply what a programmer does when putting bits of code together into a program or an application. In this view, any legitimate programming language construct is a unit of composition; and composition is simply joining these constructs together using some other construct (e.g. sequencing) defined in the programming language. We call this the 'programming view' of composition.

Meaningful units of composition in the programming view include *functions* in functional languages, *procedures* in imperative languages, *classes* [Szyperski (2002b)] and *aspects* [Kiczales *et al.* (1997)] in object-oriented and aspect-oriented languages respectively.

Clearly the 'programming view' represents programming-in-the-small. To equate composition with this view, however, is to overlook many issues that are significant for software engineering, such as *reuse* and *systematic* or *automated construction*.

3.1.2 The Construction View

A higher-level view of composition is the view that software composition is "the process of constructing applications by interconnecting software components through their plugs" [Nierstrasz and Dami (1995)]. The primary motivation here is *systematic construction*.

We call this view the 'construction view' of composition. It is at a higher level of abstraction than the 'programming view': it typically uses *scripting languages* [Ousterhout (1998)] to connect pre-existing program units together. The 'construction view' thus represents programming-in-the-large [DeRemer and Kron (1976)], as opposed to programming-in-the-small.

In the 'construction view', the units of composition are referred to as components, but these are only loosely defined as software units with plugs, which are interaction or connection points. Consequently, components may be any software units that can be scripted together by glue. For example, components may be modules glued by module interaction languages [Prieto-Diaz (1991)], or Java Beans composed by Piccola [Achermann *et al.* (2001)], and so on.

System designs in the 'construction view' are represented by software architectures [Shaw and Garlan (1996); Bass *et al.* (2012)]. A software architecture contains components and their inter-connections.

Although the 'construction view' hints at software reuse (via components) [Nierstrasz (1995); Nierstrasz and Meijler (1995); Sametinger (1997)], it does not explicitly show how reuse occurs. In particular, it does not assume that components are supplied by third parties (and pre-exist in a repository). Software architectures similarly do not make any assumptions about component reuse.

3.1.3 The CBD View

To define components precisely, we should define them in the context of a *component model* [(2001); Lau and Wang (2007)]. A component model defines what components are (their syntax and semantics) and what composition operators can be used to compose them (Chapter 4). Thus in [(2001)] a software component is defined as "a software element that conforms to a component model and can be independently deployed and composed without modification according to a composition standard".

The advent of CBD [Broy *et al.* (1998); (2001); Szyperski *et al.* (2002)] brought about a sharper focus on not only component models (different kinds of components and composition mechanisms), but also repositories of (pre-existing) components and component reuse from such repositories. Thus CBD is motivated by systematic construction as well as *reuse* of *(pre-existing) third-party compo-nents*. We call this the 'CBD view'; it extends the 'construction view', by the additional emphasis on component models as well as reuse of third-party compo-nents.

Software architectures also subscribe to the 'CBD view', in addition to the 'construction view', in the sense that an architecture description language (ADL) [Clements (1996); Medvidovic and Taylor (2000)] could be considered to be a component model, with architectural units as components, and port connection as a composition mechanism for such components. However, in contrast to the 'CBD view', software architectures do not always assume or make use of third-party components or repositories of such components, as we remarked earlier.

In the 'CBD view', units of composition are components as defined in the chosen component model.

Generic components (Fig. 2.1) are composed by matching their required and provided services. Objects (Fig. 2.4(a)) cannot be 'composed' this way, since they do not specify their required services; rather, they 'compose' by direct method calls. Architectural units (Fig. 2.4(b)) compose by connecting their (compatible) ports. Encapsulated components *Encapsulated component* (Fig. 2.4(c)) cannot connect directly; rather they need to be coordinated by exogenous composition connectors, see e.g. [Lau and Ornaghi (2009); Velasco Elizondo and Lau (2010)].

Finally, it is worth re-iterating that the boundaries between these views are not cut and dried. In particular, the construction view and the CBD view overlap, as already pointed out. This is mainly due to the generic nature of components de-fined in the construction view, which loosely covers components in all the current component models.

3.2 Software Composition Mechanisms

Now we survey composition mechanisms that have been defined in all three views. As already mentioned, we view a unit of composition as a software unit that de-fines *behaviour*, and composition mechanisms as ways of building larger units of behaviour. Since it does not make much sense to consider composition mech-anisms that are only unary in arity, our normal assumption is that composition mechanisms are (at least) *binary* in arity.

Composition mechanisms in all three views fall into four general categories: (i) containment; (ii) extension; (iii) connection; and (iv) coordination. We now briefly define and explain each category, using generic units of composition, and, for elucidation and illustration, we compare and contrast the category with corre-sponding UML mechanisms.

3.2.1 *Containment*

Containment refers to putting units of behaviour inside the definition of a larger unit. This is illustrated in Fig. 3.1(a), where U3 contains U1 and U2. Containment is thus *nested definition*. The behaviour of the container unit is defined in terms

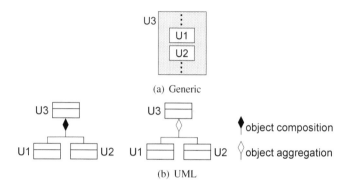

(a) Generic

(b) UML

Fig. 3.1 Containment.

of that of the contained units, but the precise nature of the containment differs from mechanism to mechanism. Examples of containment are nested definitions of functions, procedures, modules and classes, as well as object composition and object aggregation.

Compared to (standard) UML, our notion of containment covers more composition mechanisms. In UML, containment is defined for classes only; object aggregation and object composition are forms of containment (Fig. 3.1(b)).

3.2.1.1 *Example*

Object composition and object aggregation in object-oriented programming are representative examples of containment. In object composition, the container object manages the life cycle of the contained objects, i.e. the latter get constructed and destroyed with the former. In contrast, in object aggregation, the life cycle of the contained objects is independent of that of the container object. This is illustrated by the C++ example in Fig. 3.2.

The compose class (Fig. 3.2(a)) *composes* two objects of the contained class managing the life cycle of two instances (first, second). Whenever an instance of compose is created, two instances (first, second) of contained are created, and their life cycle is managed by compose. In contrast, the aggregate class (Fig. 3.2(b)) only *aggregates* two objects of the contained

```
class contained
{• • •}
class compose
{
 public:
 • • •
 private:
   contained first;
   contained second;
};
```

(a) Object composition

```
class aggregate
{
 public:
 • • •
 void setContained(contained *,contained *);
 private:
   contained *first;
   contained *second;
};
void aggregate::setContained(contained *c1,contained *c2)
{ first=c1; second=c2; }
```

(b) Object aggregation

Fig. 3.2   Containment: Composing objects by object composition and object aggregation.

class, because it only contains pointers to them. Class `aggregate` does not manage the life cycle of instances pointed by (`first`, `second`). Whenever an instance of `aggregate` is created, no instances of `contained` are created. Such instances have to be created by a class holding a reference to an instance of `aggregate` by passing their addresses by invoking the `setContained` method in `aggregate`.

3.2.2   *Extension*

Extension refers to defining the behaviour of a unit by extending that of at least two other units of composition. This is illustrated in Fig. 3.3(a). Examples of

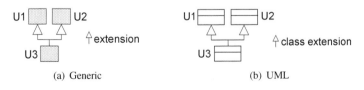

(a) Generic   (b) UML

Fig. 3.3   Extension.

extension include multiple inheritance in object-oriented programming, aspect weaving [Kiczales *et al.* (2001)] in aspect-oriented programming, subject composition [Ossher *et al.* (1996)] (or correspondence-combination, or superimposition [Apel and Lengauer (2008)]) in subject-oriented programming and feature composition [Prehofer (2002)] in feature-oriented programming (Fig. 3.13).

Multiple inheritance can be defined as a composition mechanism that extends multiple classes (e.g. U1 and U2 in Fig. 3.3(b)) into another class (U3) that inherits from these classes.

Aspect weaving can be defined as a (binary) composition mechanism that extends a class (say U1 in Fig. 3.3(a)) and an aspect (U2) into another class (U3) that is the result of weaving U2 into U1. (Of course U3 is just the new version of U1.)

Similarly, subject composition and feature composition can be defined as composition mechanisms that extend multiple subjects and features respectively (e.g. U1 and U2 in Fig. 3.3(a)) into another subject or feature (U3) that is the result of superimposition between these subjects or features.

Compared to UML, our notion of extension covers more composition mechanisms. In UML, extension is used to define inheritance for classes only, and the only composition mechanism based on extension is multiple inheritance (Fig. 3.3(b)). Other extension mechanisms, namely aspect weaving, subject composition and feature composition, can only be represented in UML as multiple inheritance if it is acceptable to represent an aspect, a subject or a feature as a class. However, if aspects, subjects and features are to be distinguished from classes, as they are intended to be, in aspect-oriented, subject-oriented and feature-oriented programming, then we cannot define aspect weaving, subject composition and feature composition as composition mechanisms in UML. In this case, in UML, aspect weaving can only be defined as single inheritance: an aspect is not a class, rather it defines what is inherited by the sub-class from a single super-class (the sub-class is the new version of the super-class).

3.2.2.1 *Example*

Aspect weaving is a representative example of the extension mechanism. An aspect [Kiczales *et al.* (1997)] defines a crosscutting concern for some base code. It can be woven with the base code to change the latter's behaviour by adding behaviour (*advice*) at various points (*join points*) in the base code specified in a *pointcut* (that identifies matching join points). Weaving is done by an aspect weaving mechanism, which is a special language processor that weaves advices[1] into a class construct. Figure 3.4 shows a simple aspect in AspectJ [Kiczales *et al.*

---

[1] As well as inter-type declarations.

(2001)] to print out Entering before executing the display method of any class with any return type, and to print out Exiting after executing the method, that is woven with a Java class application. The pointcut log specifies the join points

```
public class application{···
  public void display(){
  System.out.println("Mode");
  }···
}

public aspect trace{
  pointcut log():
    execution(public **.display());
  before():log(){//before advice
    System.out.println("Entering ---");}
  after()returning:log(){//after advice
    System.out.println("Exiting ---");}
}
```

Output before weaving: Output after weaving:
Mode   Entering ---
                                                                          Mode
                                                                          Exiting ---

Fig. 3.4   Extension: Composing an aspect with a class by aspect weaving.

as before and after the execution of any display method. The aspect trace thus extends the behaviour of the class application class.

3.2.3   *Connection*

Connection refers to defining a behaviour that is an interaction between the behaviours of multiple units. This is illustrated in Fig. 3.5. Such interaction is

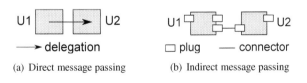

(a) Direct message passing   (b) Indirect message passing

Fig. 3.5   Connection.

effected by the units either directly or indirectly invoking each other's behaviour. Connection is thus *message passing*, and as such it induces tight coupling between units that send messages to each other. Examples of connection include object delegation and port connection between architectural units (Fig. 3.13).

Direct message passing (Fig. 3.5(a)) is a form of delegation. An example is object delegation [Ostermann and Mezini (2001)]. Objects directly invoke each other's methods, i.e. they connect by direct method calls, or delegation. This is illustrated for three objects A, B, C in Fig. 3.6. In general, an object could call

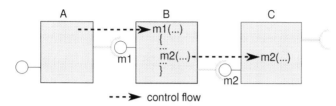

Fig. 3.6   Connection by direct method call.

any number of methods in another object. This is true for an arbitrary assembly of connected objects.

Indirect message passing (Fig. 3.5(b)) is done via plugs in the units. Plugs provide input/output points via which units can communicate. An example of indirect message passing is architectural units connected via their ports. An

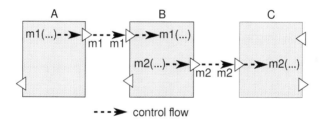

Fig. 3.7   Connection by indirect message passing.

architectural unit has ports, for input and output, which can be linked to the ports of other architectural units by connectors. Architectural units invoke each other's behaviour by messages passed via their ports. Figure 3.7 shows three units linked via (some of) their ports. Connected ports have to be compatible of course.

Compared to UML, our notion of connection covers more composition mechanisms. In UML, connection is only defined for UML2.0 components, not for classes. In UML2.0 [OMG (2003)], components are architectural units with input ports that are *required interfaces* (for *required services*) and output ports that are *provided interfaces* (for *provided services*). Figure 3.8 shows a UML2.0 component. Port connection is done by using *assembly* connectors, and port forwarding or exporting is done by using *delegation* connectors, illustrated in Fig. 3.9.

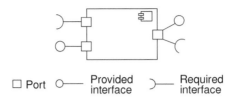

Fig. 3.8   UML2.0 component.

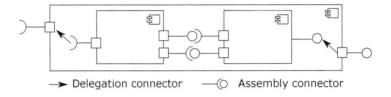

Fig. 3.9   Connection in UML2.0.

Somewhat ironically, UML has no notation for object delegation. Association between classes can only express relationships between classes, but not method calls between objects.

3.2.3.1 *Example*

We have already explained object delegation and port connection for architectural units (see Figs. 3.6 and 3.7). Here we give a more detailed example of port connection. Fig. 3.10 shows the composition of two architectural units A and B in ArchJava (Section 6.2). Fig. 3.10(a) shows the code of the architectural units while Fig. 3.10(b) shows their composition. Port y of A is connected to port x of B. Port x of A and ports n, m, y of B are forwarded (by delegation connectors) as ports n, m, y of the composite AB by gluing the former to the latter. Forwarding different ports would result in a different composite with different ports. In general, a port may have multiple services, which may be either required or provided services; in this example we have only used ports with a single service.

3.2.4 *Coordination*

Coordination refers to defining a behaviour that results from coordinating the behaviours of multiple units. This is illustrated in Fig. 3.11. The coordination is performed by a coordinator which communicates with the units via a control and/or a data channel. The units themselves do not communicate directly with one another.

```
component class A{
  port x{requires int readNum();}
  port y{provides int add();}
  port n{requires char readTxt();}
  port m{provides void printChar();}
  //implementation of provided methods
  . . .
}
component class B{
  port x{requires int add();}
  port y{provides int sqr();}
  port n{requires char readTxt();}
  port m{provides void printChar();}
  //implementation of provided methods
  . . .
}
component class AB{
  port x{requires int readNum();}
  port y{provides int sqr();}
  port n{requires char readTxt();}
  port m{provides void printChar();}
  private final A a=new A();
  private final B b=new B();
  connect a.y,b.x;
  glue n to b.n;
  glue x to a.x;
  glue m to b.m;
  glue y to b.y;
}
```

(a) Architectural units

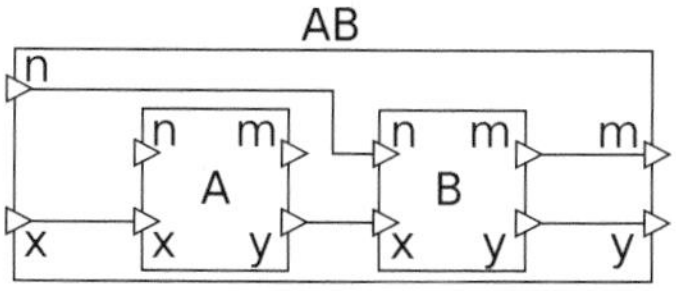

(b) Composition

Fig. 3.10   Connection: Composing architectural units by port connection.

Coordination thus removes all coupling between the units, in contrast to connection, which induces tight coupling through message passing. Examples of coordination are data coordination using tuple spaces [Gelernter and Carriero (1992)], data coordination using data connectors [Arbab (2004)] for parallel processes or active components, control coordination using orchestration [Erl (2005)] for (web) services, and control coordination using exogenous composition for encapsulated components (Fig. 3.13).

Tuple spaces are used in coordination languages to coordinate parallel processes, by storing and sharing typed data objects (tuples) between the processes. In contrast to connection mechanisms, these processes communicate only with the tuple space, but not directly or indirectly with each other.

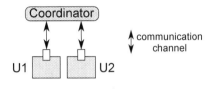

Fig. 3.11   Coordination.

Data connectors are data channels that coordinate the data flow between the ports of active components, thus separating the data flow from computation. The components execute their own threads, consuming data values on their input ports and putting data values on their output ports. The components do not communicate directly with each other. The flow of data values is defined by the data channels between them.

In control coordination, control connectors coordinate the control flow between passive components. The components do not have their own threads, and are executed only when control reaches them from the control connectors. Control coordination thus separates control flow from computation. is a representative example of coordination. A web service [Erl (2005)] provides a set of operations that can be invoked by users via its WSDL (web service description language) [Christensen *et al.* (2001)] interface (with web enabled protocols). A sequence of invocations can be defined as a workflow, in a workflow language like BPEL (business process execution language) [OASIS (2007)], and when the workflow is executed on a workflow engine, the invocations take place. Such a workflow is called an *orchestration*. Thus orchestration is a composition mechanism for web services.

This is illustrated in Fig. 3.12 for two web services $WS1$ and $WS2$. Figure 3.12(a) shows how a BPEL process orchestrates the two web services, and Fig. 3.12(b) shows the workflow created by this orchestration. The workflow, depicted by an activity diagram, is defined as a BPEL process: it invokes operation X in $WS1$, and then invokes either operation Y in $WS1$ or operation Z in $WS2$ depending on whether condition $c1$ or $c2$ holds, and then terminates. Thus, orchestration coordinates the invocation of operations in $WS1$ and $WS2$. Figure 3.12(c) shows the code for this BPEL process.

3.2.5   *The Complete Survey*

Our complete survey of software composition mechanisms is structured according to the above four categories (and the three views) and is shown in Fig. 3.13.

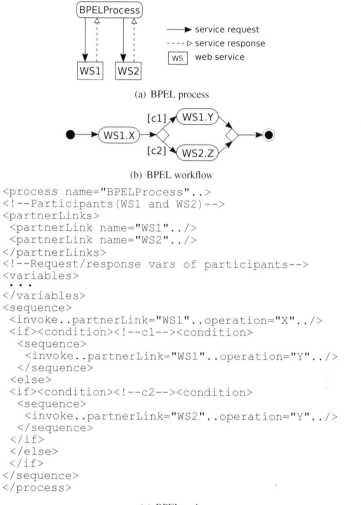

(a) BPEL process

(b) BPEL workflow

```
<process name="BPELProcess"..>
<!--Participants(WS1 and WS2)-->
<partnerLinks>
 <partnerLink name="WS1"../>
 <partnerLink name="WS2"../>
</partnerLinks>
<!--Request/response vars of participants-->
<variables>
 ...
</variables>
<sequence>
 <invoke..partnerLink="WS1"..operation="X"../>
 <if><condition><!--c1--><condition>
  <sequence>
   <invoke..partnerLink="WS1"..operation="Y"../>
  </sequence>
 <else>
 <if><condition><!--c2--><condition>
  <sequence>
   <invoke..partnerLink="WS2"..operation="Y"../>
  </sequence>
 </if>
 </else>
 </if>
</sequence>
</process>
```

(c) BPEL code

Fig. 3.12 Coordination: composing web services by orchestration.

The Containment category contains function nesting, procedure nesting, class nesting, object composition and object aggregation, and module nesting.

The Extension category contains multiple (class) inheritance, mixin-inheritance [Bracha and Cook (1990)], mixin-class inheritance, trait composition [Ducasse *et al.* (2006)], trait-class composition, subject composition, feature composition, (aspect) weaving and invasive composition.

Unit of Composition	Composition Mechanism			
	Containment	Extension	Connection	Coordination
Function	Function nesting		Higher-order function Function call	
Procedure	Procedure nesting		Procedure call	
Class	Class nesting Object composition Object aggregation	Multiple inheritance	Object delegation	
Mixin		Mixin inheritance		
Mixin/Class		Mixin-class inheritance		
Trait		Trait composition	Trait composition	
Trait/Class		Trait-class composition	Trait-class composition	
Subject		Subject composition		
Feature		Feature composition		
Aspect/Class		Weaving		
Module	Module nesting		Module connection	
Architectural unit			Port connection	
Fragment box		Invasive composition	Invasive composition	
Process			Channels	Data coordination
Web service				Orchestration (Control coordination)
Encapsulated component				Exogenous composition (Control coordination)

(Left-side vertical labels: Programming View, CBD View. Right-side vertical label: Construction View.)

Fig. 3.13   Categories of software composition mechanisms.

The Connection category contains higher-order function, function call, procedure call, object delegation, trait composition, trait-class composition, module connection, port connection, invasive composition, and (process [Hoare (2005)]) channels.

The Coordination category includes data coordination, (web service) orchestration and exogenous composition (of encapsulated components).

Our survey shows some interesting characteristics of the three views, and the composition mechanisms therein. Each view is based on a particular kind of unit of composition. In the programming view, units of composition do not have plugs. In the construction view, units of composition have plugs: modules have interaction points as plugs; architectural units have ports as plugs; fragment boxes [Aß-mann (2003)] have hooks as plugs; processes have channels as plugs. In the CBD view, units of composition have proper interfaces for composition: web services have WSDL interfaces; encapsulated components have interfaces for exogenous composition.

The boundaries between views are of course not clear cut. As we pointed out in Section 3.1, the construction and the CBD views overlap. This is evident in Fig. 3.13. The construction view also overlaps slightly with the programming view. A module could be a unit of composition in the programming view. However, modules with interfaces do have plugs for interacting with other modules; so a module is also a unit of composition in the construction view. Another example is a feature. A feature in feature-oriented programming does not have plugs, but a feature in the Genvoca model [Batory *et al.* (1994)] does have plugs; such a feature would be a unit of composition in the construction view.

In each view, there is a predominant kind of composition mechanism, except the programming view, where all composition mechanisms except coordination are used. In the construction view, without the assumption of third-party components, the predominant composition mechanism is connection. This reflects the primary concern of constructing larger pieces of software from smaller pieces. The fact that modules use nesting betrays its programming view roots. In the CBD view, with the presumption of (pre-existing) third-party components, the predominant composition mechanism is coordination. This is due to the assumption of third-party components: web services are assumed to be available on web servers, while encapsulated components are assumed to be in repositories provided by third parties.

3.3 Algebraic Composition Mechanisms

Our survey is not based on any desiderata for composition mechanisms, but it does provide a comprehensive source of information for further analysis of the mechanisms in terms of desirability criteria. In this section we show a taxonomy based on a desideratum for CBD, namely systematic construction. We will show that mechanisms that are *algebraic* meet this desideratum, and identify such mechanisms.

When a composition mechanism is applied to units of composition of a given type, the resulting piece of software may or may not be another unit of composition of the same type. If it is, then it can be used in further composition; composition mechanisms that produce units of composition of the same type as the composed units of composition are *algebraic*. Algebraic composition mechanisms are good for hierarchical composition (and therefore systematic construction), since each composition is carried out in the same manner regardless of the level of the construction hierarchy. Indeed in the 'construction view', such mechanisms are deemed the most desirable since they can constitute a component algebra [Achermann and Nierstrasz (2005)].

We only consider one-sorted algebra, not many-sorted algebras, where 'algebraic' would mean the resulting unit is of the same type as at least one of the composed units. In practice, in any programming paradigm, there is usually only one pre-dominant, paradigm-defining sort, e.g. object-oriented programming, service-oriented programming, etc.

Composition Mechanism				Algebraic?
Containment	Extension	Connection	Coordination	
	Mixin-class inheritance	Function call	Data coordination	✗
		Procedure call		
	Trait-class composition	Module connection		
		Object delegation	Orchestration	
	Weaving	Trait-class composition		
Function nesting	Multiple inheritance	Higher-order function	Exogenous composition	✓
Procedure nesting	Mixin inheritance	Trait composition		
Module nesting	Trait composition	Port connection		
Class nesting	Subject composition	Invasive composition		
Object composition	Feature composition			
Object aggregation	Invasive composition	Channels		

Fig. 3.14　Algebraic versus non-algebraic composition mechanisms.

Analysing the mechanisms in our survey in Fig 3.13, we arrive at the taxonomy of algebraic versus non-algebraic mechanisms in Fig. 3.14.

In the Containment category, all the mechanisms are algebraic, since the composite is always the same type as the composed units.

In the Extension category, some mechanisms are algebraic, while some are not. Multiple inheritance yields a class from two classes and is therefore algebraic. Similarly, mixin inheritance, subject composition and feature composition are algebraic. Trait composition can be done by either extension or connection, but it is always algebraic since it always yields another trait. Invasive composition performs both extension (by overwriting) and connection (via hooks), but it is always algebraic because it always yields another fragment box.

Mixin-class inheritance and weaving yield, respectively a class from a mixin and a class, and a class from an aspect and a class, and are therefore not algebraic. Trait-class composition falls into both the Extension and Connection categories, depending on whether the trait composition involved is done by extension or connection, but trait-class composition is always non-algebraic since it yields a class from a trait and a class.[2]

---

[2]Our classification of subject composition as algebraic, and aspect weaving as non-algebraic, mirrors

Like the Extension category, in the Connection category, some mechanisms are algebraic and some are not. A higher-order function composes functions and yields a function, and is therefore algebraic. So is port connection, which composes architectural units and yields an architectural unit. Channels connecting processes create new processes, and are therefore algebraic.

A function call returns a pair of functions rather than a single function, and is therefore non-algebraic. Similarly, procedure call, module connection, and object delegation are non-algebraic.

Finally, in the Coordination category, only exogenous composition as in X-MAN (Section 7.1) is algebraic, since the composition of two encapsulated components always yields an encapsulated component. In X-MAN (Fig. 3.15), the

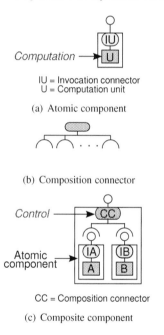

IU = Invocation connector
U = Computation unit

(a) Atomic component

(b) Composition connector

CC = Composition connector

(c) Composite component

Fig. 3.15   Exogenous composition in X-MAN.

components are encapsulated (Fig. 2.4(c)). There are two basic types of components: (i) *atomic* and (ii) *composite*. An atomic component (Fig. 3.15(a)) consists of a *computation* unit (U) and an *invocation connector* (IU). A computation unit contains a set of methods which do not invoke methods in the computation units

---

the dichotomy between symmetric and asymmetric aspect mechanisms [Harrison *et al.* (2002); Kojarski and Lorenz (2006)] in aspect-oriented software development.

of other components; it therefore encapsulates computation. An invocation connector passes control (and input parameters) received from outside the component to the computation unit to invoke a chosen method, and after the execution of method passes control (and results) back to whence it came, outside the component. It therefore encapsulates control. A composite component (Fig. 3.15(c)) is built from atomic components by using a *composition connector* (Fig. 3.15(b)). Such a connector encapsulates a control structure, e.g. sequencing, branching, or looping, that connects the sub-components to the interface of the composite component. Since the atomic components encapsulate computation and control, so does the composite component. Encapsulated components therefore encapsulate control (and computation) at every level of composition. Figure 3.15 clearly shows that exogenous composition is algebraic: exogenous composition of encapsulated components always yields another encapsulated component. The composition connector provides the interface of the composite, which is derived directly from the interfaces of the composed components.

Data coordination is not algebraic since it does not yield a single process; rather it yields the same set of processes (either sharing a tuple space or connected by data connectors). Orchestration of web services is not algebraic since the result of an orchestration is a workflow, rather than a web service, as we showed in Section 3.2.5. Of course the workflow could be turned into web service, by creating a WSDL interface for it, but this would require an extra step after orchestration. Indeed, some BPEL editors force the user to take this extra step in order to make the orchestration executable as a web service.

3.4   Mathematical Composition Operators

Another desideratum for CBD is that composition mechanisms should be automatable. A composition is automatable if it can be explicitly defined as a mathematical composition operator, i.e. like a mathematical function, that can be defined and then applied to arbitrary arguments, i.e. units of composition of specified types. For example, a higher-order function $h : X \to Z$ that composes two functions $f : X \to Y$ and $g : Y \to Z$ (where X, Y, Z are types) can be defined explicitly in terms of f and g as $h(x) = g(f(x))$. The mathematical operator h can be used to compose any two functions with type signatures $X \to Y$ and $Y \to Z$.

Applying a mathematical composition operator does not require any glue that has to be constructed manually. With mathematical composition operators defined from algebraic composition mechanisms, we can automate hierarchical composition. In this section, we show a taxonomy of algebraic composition mechanisms

Algebraic Composition Mechanism				Composition operator ?
Containment	Extension	Connection	Coordination	
	Mixin inheritance	Higher-order function	Exogenous composition	✓
	Subject composition			
Function nesting	Multiple inheritance	Trait composition		
Procedure nesting				
Module nesting	Trait composition	Port connection		✗
Class nesting	Feature composition	Invasive composition		
Object composition				
Object aggregation	Invasive composition	Channels		

Fig. 3.16   Algebraic composition mechanisms as mathematical operators.

that can be defined as mathematical operators versus those that cannot. This taxonomy is shown in Fig. 3.16.

In the Containment category, no mechanism can be defined as a mathematical operator, since nesting can be done in arbitrary ways.

In the Extension category, multiple inheritance, trait composition, and feature composition, all perform extension that may require glue for conflict resolution and overriding in general, and therefore cannot be defined as mathematical operators. Invasive composition requires glue for both extension and connection, and therefore cannot be defined as mathematical operators.

By contrast, mixin inheritance never requires glue, since it performs extension in a fixed manner. A mixin M is a set of methods, and can be defined as a record $\{f_1 \mapsto m_1, \ldots, f_n \mapsto m_n\}$ with fields $f_1, \ldots, f_n$ whose values are the signatures $m_1, \ldots, m_n$ of M's methods. Mixin inheritance can be defined as record combination, which is a binary operation $\oplus$ [Bracha and Cook (1990)] such that $M_1 \oplus M_2$, for any M_1 and M_2 yields a new mixin M_3 which is a new record with the fields from M_1 and M_2, where the value for each field is the value from the left argument M_1 (or the right argument M_2) in case the same field is present in both records.

Figure 3.17 shows an example in MixedJava [Flatt *et al.* (1999)]: mixin A with methods $m1, m2, m5$; $m5$ prints the message 'Alpha'. Mixin B has methods $m3, m4, m5$; $m5$ prints the message 'Beta'. The first composition expression generates a composite mixin AB, in which A's $m5$ overrides B's $m5$. Similarly, the second composition expression generates a composite mixin BA, in which B's $m5$ overrides A's $m5$.

Similarly, it is possible to define simple correspondence-combination mathematical operators for composing arbitrary subjects, e.g. a simple 'merge-and-overwrite' operator. However, it is difficult to define mathematical operators

```
mixin A{
  m1(){• • •} m2(){• • •} m5(){//print Alpha}
}

mixin B{
  m3(){• • •} m4(){• • •} m5(){//print Beta}
}

//two composition expressions
mixin AB = A compose B;
mixin BA = B compose A;

mixin AB{
  m1(){• • •} m2(){• • •} m3(){• • •} m4(){• • •}
  m5(){//print Alpha}
}

mixin BA{
  m1(){• • •} m2(){• • •} m3(){• • •} m4(){• • •}
  m5(){//print Beta}
}
```

Fig. 3.17   Mixin!inheritance.

for complex correspondence-combination mechanisms that can compose arbitrary subjects.

In the Connection category, for any two given traits and two architectural units, respectively, there are in principle many different possible pairs of matching services and compatible ports, and each permutation of possible pairs gives rise to a composition operator. Thus composing traits and architectural units by connection is necessarily done in an *ad hoc* manner, and cannot be defined as mathematical operators. Similarly, for any two given processes, there are many different possible channels for connecting them. Thus composing processes by channels connection cannot be defined as mathematical operators.

In the Coordination category, exogenous composition can be defined as mathematical composition operators (connectors), as we have already seen in the previous section.

Finally, the taxonomy in Fig. 3.16 is a sub-taxonomy of the taxonomy (Fig. 3.14) presented in the previous section. Together they form the taxonomy that identifies desirable composition mechanisms for CBD. Figure 3.16 shows that these mechanisms are mixin-inheritance, subject composition and higher-order function (from the programming view) and exogenous composition (from the CBD view). Of these, only exogenous composition is being used in CBD. Apart from exogenous composition, current component models predominantly use object delegation and port connection (for architectural units).

Discussion and Further Reading

Various categories for software composition mechanisms have been proposed before. Nierstrasz and Dami [Nierstrasz and Dami (1995)] suggest three different types of compositional paradigms for components (static abstractions with plugs): (i) functional composition, (ii) blackboard composition and (iii) extensibility. Components are seen as (mathematical) functions from input values to output values. In functional composition, components are composed like (mathematical) functions. This corresponds to the higher-order function mechanism in our Connection category. Blackboard composition is data sharing by components, and is therefore data coordination in our Coordination category. Extensibility is not a separate mechanism, but part of functional composition; it allows individual components to be extended (by single inheritance), and requires any such extension to be preserved in any functional composition involving extended components. Nierstrasz and Dami do not have our Containment and Extension categories.

Sametinger [Sametinger (1997)] categorises software composition mechanisms into two basic forms: (i) internal and (ii) external. In internal composition mechanisms, composed units become inherent parts of the composite, e.g. when source code is compiled and linked to an executable file. This corresponds to our Containment category in a coarse-grained way; it is not clear whether object aggregation is internal. In external composition mechanisms, composed units execute independently and communicate with other composed units by interprocess communication techniques. This covers our Connection and Coordination categories, but again in a very coarse-grained manner. It is not clear which of these forms our Extension category belongs to.

Sommerville (2004b) defines three types of composition mechanisms for architectural units: (i) sequential, (ii) hierarchical and (iii) additive. In sequential composition, the 'provided' interfaces of the units are linked by glue code that executes their services in sequence; what happens to the 'required' ports is not defined. Without 'required' ports, this mechanism seems to be a control coordination mechanism, and seems to be non-algebraic. Hierarchical composition is the same as port connection in our Connection category. Additive composition simply yields a composite whose interface is the set of the interfaces of the components. This is a degenerate form of port connection in which only delegation connectors are used (to forward ports to the composite). Sommerville does not have the Containment or Extension categories since he only addresses architectural units. He also seems not to have the Coordination category.

Szyperski [Szyperski (2002b)] classifies software composition approaches into two categories: (i) symmetric and (ii) asymmetric. Symmetric means the definition of composition is located in (one of) the composed components, e.g. object delegation, while asymmetric means the location of composition definition is outside in a neutral place, e.g. container-based composition like in EJB. These are coarse-grained categories, with symmetric covering our Containment, Extension and Connection categories, while asymmetric corresponds to our Coordination category.

Mehta *et al.* (2000) define composition mechanisms for components as connectors, and categorise them into connectors for: (i) communication (ii) coordination (iii) conversion and (iv) facilitation. Communication connectors transfer data, whilst coordination connectors transfer control, between components. These connectors belong to our Connection category, since they compose components by message passing. Conversion connectors convert the interaction required by one component to that provided by another, e.g. conversion of data format; thus they are adaptors. Our categories do not include adaptors; we do not consider them to be composition mechanisms since they are unary operators. Facilitation connectors provide mechanisms for facilitating and optimizing component interactions. They do not feature in our categories.

The only work related to our taxonomy for CBD is that of Chaudron [Chaudron (2001)]. He does not propose any taxonomy, but he does define desiderata for composition mechanisms for CBD. Interestingly, Chaudron's desiderata support our taxonomy for CBD. Three of his criteria which are relevant here state that: (i) composition mechanisms should be exogenous to components, i.e. not built into the components themselves; (ii) composition mechanisms should provide separate mechanisms for dealing with control flow and data flow; (iii) composition languages should provide means for building higher level, larger-granularity composition abstractions. (i) and (ii) support our classification of exogenous composition (of encapsulated components) as desirable for CBD (Fig. 3.16), while (iii) supports our choice of algebraic mechanisms as desirable for CBD (Fig. 3.14).

For practical development, we will always need to use a combination of different kinds of components and composition mechanisms. Non-algebraic mechanisms or mechanisms that cannot be defined as mathematical operators may be better for top-level system design. On the other hand, given a top-level architectural design, it may be better to provide all its required services by designing the desired composites using mathematical composition operators that can be applied automatically.

We have not addressed run-time or dynamic composition, e.g. *proximity-based* composition (objects in a context may be automatically connected) [Szyperski (2002a)], and *data-driven* composition [Szyperski (2002a)].

Finally, we agree with Szyperski [Szyperski (2002a,b)] that for CBD the 'universe of composition' is as yet largely unexplored. Our work here is a response to his 'call-to-arms' [Szyperski (2002a)].

Acknowledgement

We thank Uwe Aßmann, Don Batory, David Lorenz, Oscar Nierstrasz, Johannes Sametinger, Clemens Szyperski and Steffen Zschaler for factual information, helpful discussions and insightful comments. We also thank Michel Chaudron for pointing out a mistake in an earlier version of our paper on the survey of composition mechanisms [Lau and Rana (2010)].

Chapter 4

Software Component Models

As we have seen in Chapter 3, there are many different kinds of units of composition that could be used as components, and each kind of unit has an associated composition mechanisms. Therefore, to define a CBD method, it is necessary to specify: (i) what components it adopts; and (ii) what composition mechanisms it uses to compose the components. The entity that defines both (i) and (ii) is called a *software component model* [Lau and Wang (2005); Lau (2006a,b); Lau and Wang (2007); Crnkovic *et al.* (2011); Lau (2014); Lau *et al.* (2014)], which we have defined as follows [Lau and Wang (2007)]:

> A *software component model* is a definition of:
>
> - the *semantics* of components;
> - the *syntax* of components;
> - the *composition* of components.

The *semantics* of components is what components are meant to be, that is, what kind of unit of composition is chosen as a component. In Section 2.1, we showed that a generally accepted view of a software component is that it is a software unit with *provided services* and *required services*, as depicted in Fig. 4.1 (which is

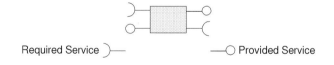

Required Service)—   —○ Provided Service

Fig. 4.1   A generic software component.

a copy of Fig. 2.1). Therefore the semantics of any unit of composition chosen as a component will be a variant of that of a generic component, with its own specialisation of the provided and required services.

The *syntax* of components determines how components are constructed and represented. Once the semantics of components has been fixed in a component model, components can be defined and constructed. The definition of components requires a *component definition language*, which may be distinct from the implementation language, i.e. programming language, for components. Clearly, for a given component definition language, components can be implemented in different programming languages. Therefore, we refer to the syntax of components as the syntax of the component definition language. In a component model, this language must be specified, whereas the implementation language(s) may be left open.

The *composition* of components defines what kinds of composition mechanisms are chosen for the components, that is, how the components are to be assembled and what the semantics of composition is. In order to define composition, we need a *component composition language*, e.g. [Lumpe *et al.* (2000)]. The composition language should have suitable semantics and syntax that are compatible with those of the components in the component model.

Clearly there are many different possible component models. In current practice, there are three main categories of component models: (i) models where components are *objects*; (ii) models where components are *architectural units*; and (iii) models where components are *encapsulated components*. Representative examples of these categories are JavaBeans [JavaBeans Specification; Oracle (2017)], architecture description languages (ADLs) [Clements (1996); Medvidovic and Taylor (2000)], and X-MAN [Lau and Tran (2012); He *et al.* (2012); di Cola *et al.* (2015)] respectively.

In this chapter, we will give an overview of these three categories of component models. In subsequent chapters, we will take a detailed look at these models.

4.1   Component Models with Objects as Components

In component models where components are *objects* (Fig. 2.4(a)) in the sense of object-oriented programming, the component definition language is the chosen object-oriented programming language, as is the component composition language. Composition is by *connection by direct message passing* (Fig. 3.5(a)), i.e. *object delegation*, in the programming language.

4.1.1 *Semantics of Components*

The semantics of a component that is an object in an object-oriented programming language is of course defined by the programming language: an object has a signature and methods that can call, and can be called by, methods in other objects. As a component, an object's methods are its provided services, as shown in Fig. 4.2

(which is a copy of Fig. 2.4(a)); whilst its required services are not specified, and hence the blurring out of the sockets in Fig. 4.2.

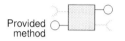

Fig. 4.2   An object as a component.

4.1.2   *Syntax of Components*

The syntax of a component, that is an object in an object-oriented programming language, is also defined by the programming language. For example, in JavaBeans [JavaBeans Specification; Oracle (2017)] a component is called a Java bean but syntactically it is just a Java class.

4.1.3   *Composition of Components*

Objects 'compose' by connection by direct message passing (Fig. 3.5(a)), i.e. by direct method call. This is illustrated in Fig. 4.3 (which is a copy of Fig. 3.6). Object A 'composes' with object B by calling the method $m1$ in B, which in turn

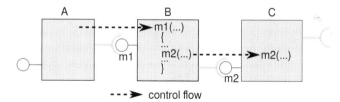

Fig. 4.3   Object composition: Connection by direct method call.

calls the method $m2$ in object C, and by so doing 'composes' objects B and C.

For example, in JavaBeans, Java beans 'compose' with one another indirectly via adapter classes that link beans via event delegation.

Object 'composition' is hard-wired in objects' code. In Fig. 4.3, object A contains the code that invokes $m1$ in object B, as indicated by the dotted arrow from A to ($m1$ in) B. The fact that A requires $m1$ is not expressed because A cannot have any required services. Similarly, ($m1$ in) object B contains the code to call $m2$ in object C, and the fact that B requires $m2$ is not expressed because B cannot have any required services.

4.2   Component Models with Architectural Units as Components

In component models where components are *architectural units* (Fig. 2.4(b)), the component definition language is an *architecture description language* (ADL) [Medvidovic and Taylor (2000)], which also provides the component composition language. Composition is by *connection by indirect message passing* (Fig. 3.5(b)).

An ADL may define components as units of design only, or as units of design and implementation. In the former case, implementation will have to be specified in some other (programming) language; an example of such an ADL is UML2.0 [OMG (2003)]. In the latter case, the ADL will be a programming language with special constructs for components and their connections; an example of such an ADL is ArchJava [Aldrich *et al.* (2001)].

4.2.1   *Semantics of Components*

A component that is an architectural unit is a generic component (Fig. 2.1) with services represented as ports as shown in Fig. 4.4 (which is a copy of Fig. 2.4(b)). Provided services are input ports (*in1* and *in2* in Fig. 4.4) and required services

Fig. 4.4   An architectural unit as a component.

are output ports (*out1* and *out2* in Fig. 4.4) respectively.

Compatible ports on different units can be linked by connectors, and in a connected pair of ports, an output port represents a required service of one unit but the provided service (and the input port) of the other unit, and vice versa.

For example, in UML2.0 [OMG (2003)], a component is an architectural unit with input ports that are required services and output ports that are provided services, as depicted in Fig. 4.5 (which is a copy of Fig. 3.8).

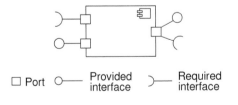

Fig. 4.5   UML2.0 component.

4.2.2 Syntax of Components

The syntax of a component that is a architectural unit is defined by the ADL. For example, in UML2.0, components are defined as UML classes with special stereotypes. The ATM component in Fig. 4.6(a) (as in Fig. 2.3) can be defined as a UML2.0 component by the UML class in Fig. 4.6(b).

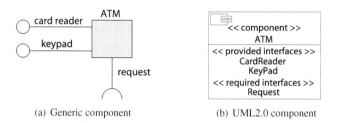

(a) Generic component   (b) UML2.0 component

Fig. 4.6   Syntax of ATM component in UML2.0.

The stereotypes <<component>>, <<provided interfaces>> and <<required interfaces>> denote a component class, methods of this class, and methods called by this class, respectively.

Examples of architectural units in ArchJava can be seen in Fig. 3.10(a).

4.2.3 Composition of Components

Architectural units compose by *connection by indirect message passing* (Fig. 3.5(b)), via port links. A remote method call is placed on a caller's output port and passed to a linked input port in the callee. The callee executes the method and returns results via the port link. This is illustrated in Fig. 4.7 (which is a copy of Fig. 3.7). Architectural unit A places a call to method $m1$ (in unit B) on

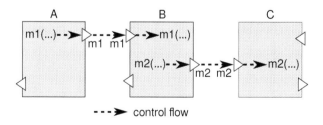

Fig. 4.7   Architectural unit composition: connection by indirect message passing.

its output port which is linked to an input port in unit B. The call is passed to B via the linked ports. Whilst executing $m1$ unit B places a call to $m2$ (in unit C) on its output port that is linked to an input port of unit C. The call is passed to C via the linked ports and executed by C. Results from call executions are passed via port links to specified destination units.

For example in UML2.0, port connection is done by using *assembly* connectors, as illustrated in Fig. 4.8 (which is a copy of Fig. 3.9). UML 2.0 also defines

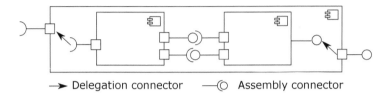

→ Delegation connector   ─◎ Assembly connector

Fig. 4.8   Composition in UML2.0.

delegation connectors for port forwarding or exporting between ports of a composite component (outer component in Fig. 4.8) and ports of the sub-components.

An example of architectural unit composition in ArchJava can be seen in Fig. 3.10.

4.3   Component Models with Encapsulated Components

In component models where components are *encapsulated components* (Fig. 2.4(c)), the component definition language could be an ADL (which defines architectural units with only provided services, and no required services), and the component composition language is either a set of pre-defined coordinators or a coordination language that can be used to define arbitrary coordination. Composition is by *coordination* (Fig. 3.11).

4.3.1   *Semantics of Components*

An encapsulated component is an architectural unit with only provided services, and no required ones, as illustrated in Fig. 4.9 (which is a copy of Fig. 2.4(c)).

Fig. 4.9   An encapsulated component.

The provided services are methods or operations provided by the component.

Thus an encapsulated component has no external dependencies. Furthermore, 'encapsulated' means that when invoked an encapsulated component does not leak control to any other component during the execution of the invoked method or operation; i.e. its computation is entirely enclosed within itself as a capsule.

For example, in X-MAN [Lau and Tran (2012); He *et al.* (2012); di Cola *et al.* (2015)], components are all encapsulated, and can be atomic or composite, as shown in Fig. 4.10. Figures 4.10(a) and 4.10(b) are copies of Figs. 3.15(a) and 3.15(c) respectively.

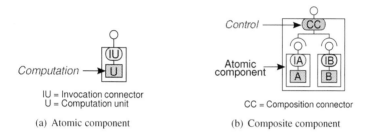

IU = Invocation connector
U = Computation unit

CC = Composition connector

(a) Atomic component   (b) Composite component

Fig. 4.10   X-MAN components.

4.3.2   *Syntax of Components*

The syntax of an encapsulated component is defined by the ADL. For example, in X-MAN, the syntax of components is defined in a graphical modelling language (in Eclipse), and captured in a graphical editor derived from this definition [di Cola *et al.* (2015)].

4.3.3   *Composition of Components*

Encapsulated components compose by coordination, as shown in Fig. 4.11, which is the same as Fig. 3.11, except the units of composition are encapsulated components.

Fig. 4.11   Encapsulated component composition: coordination.

For example, in X-MAN, coordination is defined by composition connectors, as shown in Fig. 4.12 (which is a copy of Fig. 7.2(b)). These connectors coordinate

Fig. 4.12   Composition connector in X-MAN.

control flow between the composed components. For example, in Fig. 4.10(b), a composition connector is used to compose two atomic components into a composite component. This composition connector coordinates control flow between the two atomic components. For instance a *sequencer* composition connector would invoke (and execute) the first atomic component and then invoke (and execute) the second atomic component.

Discussion and Further Reading

A tutorial on component models can be found in [Lau (2014); Lau *et al.* (2014)]. An older tutorial can be found in [Lau (2006a,b)], with further details in [Lau and Wang (2006)].

Acknowledgement

We wish to thank Ivica Crnkovic, David Garlan, Dirk Muthig, Oscar Nierstrasz, Bastiaan Schonhage and Kurt Wallnau for information and helpful discussions.

Chapter 5

Component Models with Objects as Components

In this chapter, we describe component models where components are objects. These models are basically defined by object-oriented programming languages in which components are objects and their composition is realised by method or event delegation. A system built from objects as components is just an object-oriented program with a *main* class.

The archetypal example of a component model with objects as components is JavaBeans (Section 5.2), in which Java objects are components (called beans), composed by event delegation.

Objects as components in component models often are bounded to some restrictions or have to satisfy certain properties. For example, in JavaBeans, a component is an object that (among other things) is serializable, and thus it is not a *plain old Java object*. Indeed the term POJO [Fowler *et al.* (2009)] is used to designate a plain old Java object not bound by any restriction other than those forced by the Java language specifications.[1]

Object-oriented programming frameworks, e.g. OSGi (Section 5.3.2), also use objects as their foundational elements, but they define larger building blocks, e.g. *bundles* in OSGi, in terms of objects. These building blocks are not components as such, since they have no composition mechanisms, but they group together interacting objects that collectively provide more coarse-grained functionality than individual objects. Therefore they are more wieldy for constructing large and complex applications in a modular manner.

Frameworks are thus akin to component models with objects as components that are composed by delegation. However, frameworks are not component models; rather they contain the latter. In this chapter, we also describe popular

---

[1]The equivalent to POJO for .NET (Section 5.3.3) is *plain old CLR object* (POCO). For PHP, it is *plain old PHP object* (POPO).

object-oriented frameworks and show how they are built on top of component models based on objects.

For each component model we describe, we will also analyse the component life cycle in that model, and compare it to the idealised component life cycle (Section 1.1), in order to see how well the component model supports the latter.

5.1   POJOs

If we use POJOs as components composed by method or event delegation, then POJOs can be considered a component model, completely defined in Java. The syntax of a POJO is just a Java class; its semantics is as shown in Fig. 4.2 and POJO composition is as shown in Fig. 4.3.

Thus component-based development using POJOs as a component model amounts to Java programming. Constructing a system requires defining and composing POJOs, i.e. classes and method calls, including one special POJO that defines the *main* class of the system.

In terms of the idealised component life cycle (Fig. 1.3), in the design phase a Java IDE is used to write all the code for the complete system, i.e. code for all the POJOs created by the programmer. The component life cycle for POJOs is

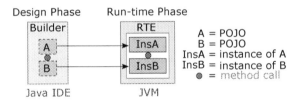

Fig. 5.1   POJOs: component life cycle.

illustrated in Fig. 5.1, which shows POJOs A and B created and composed by the user in the Java IDE in the design phase.

There is no deployment phase, as all the code has been written in the design phase, and is ready for execution on a Java virtual machine (JVM), which provides the run-time environment. The composition (by method calls) between the POJO instances at run-time is the same as that between POJOs defined in the design phase.

5.2   JavaBeans

In JavaBeans [Englander (1997); Weerawarana *et al.* (2001)] a component is a bean, which is a Java object with some prescribed properties: (i) it implements the interface *Serializable*; (ii) it has a 0-argument constructor (also known as a nullary constructor); and (iii) it allows access to its private attributes only by getter and setter methods.

Figure 5.2 outlines Java beans for an ATM and a bank. The ATM bean implements *Serializable* and has a nullary constructor *ATM( )*. It has a setter method for the attribute *CardReader reader*. It provides a *withdraw* method. The Bank

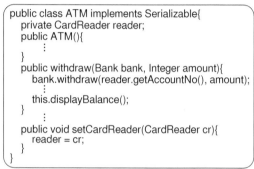

```
public class ATM implements Serializable{
    private CardReader reader;
    public ATM(){
        ⋮
    }
    public withdraw(Bank bank, Integer amount){
        bank.withdraw(reader.getAccountNo(), amount);
        ⋮
        this.displayBalance();
    }
        ⋮
    public void setCardReader(CardReader cr){
        reader = cr;
    }
}
```

ATM Bean

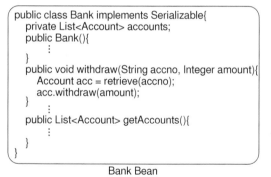

```
public class Bank implements Serializable{
    private List<Account> accounts;
    public Bank(){
        ⋮
    }
    public void withdraw(String accno, Integer amount){
        Account acc = retrieve(accno);
        acc.withdraw(amount);
    }
        ⋮
    public List<Account> getAccounts(){
        ⋮
    }
}
```

Bank Bean

Fig. 5.2   Examples of Java beans.

bean implements *Serializable* and has a nullary constructor *Bank( )*. It has a getter method for the attribute *List⟨Accounts⟩ accounts*. It also provides a *withdraw* method.

In JavaBeans, beans are constructed in a visual builder, which provides a container that houses and manages the beans. Beans in a container can be composed by linking an event generated in a source bean to a method in a target bean. The container automatically creates event adaptor objects that provide the link. This is depicted in Fig. 5.3.The event adaptor object listens for and handles the specified

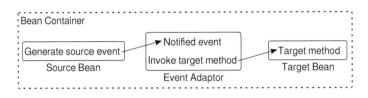

Fig. 5.3   JavaBeans: components and composition.

event generated by the source bean. When the event occurs, the event adaptor object is notified and it invokes the specified method in the target bean.

Figure 5.4 shows examples of Java beans and their composition. It depicts a simplified ATM system consisting of the composition of two beans: ATM and Bank. The two beans are composed by the event adaptor on the notification of a *withdraw* event. When provided with the account number and the required amount, the event adaptor invokes the *withdraw* method exposed by the Bank bean.

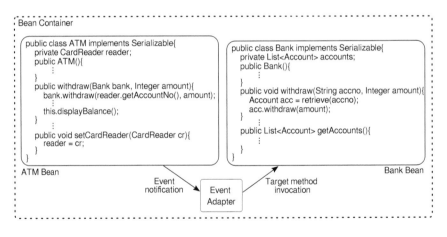

Fig. 5.4   JavaBeans: ATM example.

In terms of the idealised component life cycle, in the design phase, beans are constructed, by writing their Java code, and manipulated in a visual bean builder tool like NetBeans. Their JAR files are hosted in a repository, such as the Palette in NetBeans [Lorenz and Petkovic (2000)]. In deployment phase, beans are retrieved (dragged) from the repository, dropped and composed in a canvas (which serves as an assembler) such as the Design Form in NetBeans. This is illustrated in Fig. 5.5. The composition of beans constitutes a complete (executable) system.

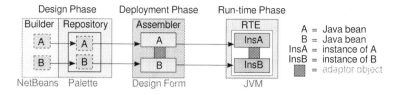

Fig. 5.5   JavaBeans: component life cycle.

Unlike POJOs, now there is no need to have a special bean with the *main* class; the container provides this.

Figure 5.5 shows clearly that in JavaBeans, composition takes place only in the deployment phase. In the design phase, beans are created individually and separately.

Finally, the most common use of beans is for graphical user interface components [Evans and Flanagan (2014)], such as buttons, boxes, and lists of the java.awt and javax.swing packages.

5.3   Object-oriented Frameworks

Object-oriented frameworks provide support for object-oriented software development. Their foundational elements are objects, and therefore they contain component models where objects are components composed by delegation.

5.3.1   *Enterprise JavaBeans*

Enterprise JavaBeans (EJB) [DeMichiel *et al.* (2001); Burke and Monson-Haefel (2006)] is a framework that provides a high-level approach to building distributed systems, by supporting server-side components that can be accessed remotely over a network by client applications.

A component in EJB is an *enterprise Java bean* (also abbreviated as EJB), which is a Java object hosted and managed by an EJB container on a J2EE server, such as Glassfish [Heffelfinger (2014)] and JBoss [Jamae and Johnson (2009)]. The EJB container serves as the execution environment for EJB components and mediates their access from remote clients. This is illustrated in Fig. 5.6.

EJB components in an EJB container are intended for collaborating in performing certain tasks for remote client applications. Their collaboration is defined by composition by delegation, both event and method delegation. Their composition does not form a complete system since none of the beans contains a *main* class. Rather, remote client applications (with their own *main* classes) can access the EJBs in the container in order to use them to perform tasks. Figure 5.6 shows

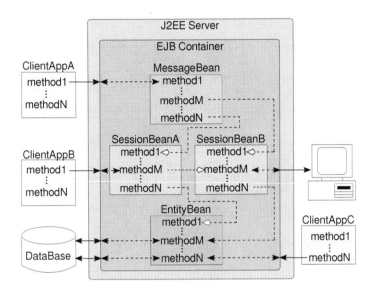

Fig. 5.6   Enterprise JavaBeans: components and composition.

three remote client applications accessing EJBs in the container to perform tasks, including accessing and updating a database remotely.

Whilst every EJB is defined by a Java class, EJBs are distinguished by their purpose. There are 3 types of EJBs: (i) *entity beans*, which model business data by providing an object-oriented view of a database's data; (ii) *session beans*, which model business processes by acting as agents performing tasks; (iii) *message-driven beans*, which model message-related business processes by acting as message listeners. Figure 5.6 shows an EJB container with one message-driven bean, two session beans and one entity bean; all composed via their methods.

A session bean represents work performed for a single client. It can be *stateful* or *stateless*. A stateful session bean is associated with a specific client, by maintaining a conversational state during the session; while a stateless session bean is not associated with any specific client. Figure 5.7 shows a stateless session bean *Bank EJB* used by an ATM client.

For every EJB, the EJB container generates a *remote interface* that exposes its capabilities, as provided by its methods. This interface provides all the methods needed for (remote) client applications to access the bean (over a network). Figure 5.7 also shows the remote interface for the *Bank EJB*, via which an *ATM Client* makes calls to the *Bank EJB*.

An entity bean models data. In the example in Fig. 5.7, assuming that account details are stored in a database, we can define an entity bean called Account that

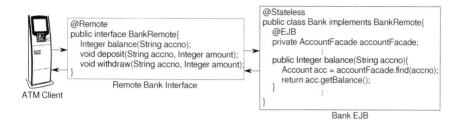

Fig. 5.7   EJB: ATM example.

consists of a Java class and a helper class. Each instance of `Account` represents the corresponding entry in the database, accessible by the *Bank EJB* via the *AccountFacade* helper.

In terms of the idealised component life cycle, in the design phase, EJBs are designed, constructed and composed in Java using a J2EE-compliant IDE (e.g. NetBeans) and the JAR files for the beans are deposited in an EJB container. This is illustrated in Fig. 5.8. The EJB container serves as a repository. However, EJBs

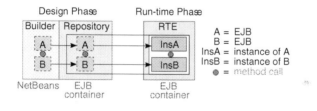

Fig. 5.8   Enterprise JavaBeans: component life cycle.

cannot be retrieved from the container for further composition; i.e. there is no deployment phase. In the run-time phase, instances of EJBs are invoked (via their remote interfaces) by client applications and executed in the EJB container, which also works as the run-time environment. The composition of the EJB instances is as defined for the EJBs in the design phase.

5.3.2   *OSGi*

The Open Services Gateway Initiative (OSGi) platform [Hall *et al.* (2011)] is a framework that brings modularity to the Java platform by offering modules defined as *bundles*. Like EJBs, bundles contain objects (POJOs) that interact to provide services to client applications. Bundles also provide services to one another. A bundle is physically distributed as a JAR file, which contains files for classes and resources. Moreover, a bundle (like a .NET assembly (Section 5.3.3)) is described by a manifest file. The latter contains information about the bundle: its symbolic name, version and imported and exported packages. Figure 5.9 shows an example of a bundle and the details of its manifest.

Fig. 5.9   An OSGi bundle.

Just as EJBs execute in an EJB container on a J2EE server, bundles execute within an OSGi compliant framework such as Equinox [McAffer *et al.* (2010)] and Felix [Gédéon (2010)].

A bundle is called a 'component' in OSGi literature. However, in terms of component models, there is no composition mechanism for bundles; so bundles are not components and OSGi is not a component model, according to our definition of component models. Correspondingly, there is no notion of composite bundles. On the other hand, classes in bundles are linked by method calls, and therefore they can be regarded as components composed by delegation. For this reason, we say that OSGi is a framework that contains a component model with objects (POJOs) as components composed by delegation in design phase. This is illustrated in Fig. 5.10.

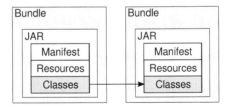

Fig. 5.10   OSGi: components and composition.

Although semantically POJO composition occurs in the design phase, an OSGi framework realises the POJOs' bindings only at run-time. Figure 5.11 shows POJOs in different bundles interacting with one another. At design time, *Bundle A* exports some services through its manifest, whilst *Bundle B* imports such services in order to get access to the exported methods. At run-time, the correct

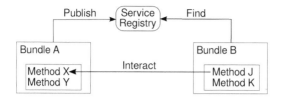

Fig. 5.11   OSGi: POJO interactions between bundles.

object references are obtained through the OSGi framework: the referring bundle (*Bundle B*) can directly call the methods of the referenced bundle (*Bundle A*).

In order to be able to dynamically locate and link bundles, the OSGi framework offers a *service registry* (Fig. 5.11) where once a bundle is started, it can register the services it offers and can also look for services offered by other bundles. The container itself executes inside a Java Virtual Machine (JVM). For this reason OSGi is sometimes referred to as a service-oriented architecture (SOA) within a JVM.

In terms of the idealised component life cycle, in the design phase in OSGi, POJOs in bundles are constructed in any editor, e.g. Eclipse. They are composed inside a bundle to provide a service exposed by the bundle. Bundles are installed in an OSGi-compliant framework, e.g. Equinox, which serves as a repository. This is illustrated in Fig. 5.12. There is no further composition and therefore there

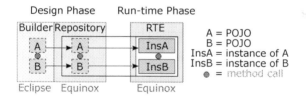

Fig. 5.12   OSGi: component life cycle.

is no deployment phase. In the run-time phase, client applications are executed and use the services provided by the bundles, by making calls to POJO instances inside the bundles via their published service interface.

5.3.3 .NET

Microsoft .NET [Esposito and Saltarello (2014); Platt (2003)] is a framework that supports object-oriented software development by providing a modular way of organising files (containing classes) into logical units. Each unit, called an *assembly*, is a binary that aggregates several physical files; in particular an assembly can contain many classes. The purpose of an assembly is to provide services (performed by their classes) to client applications, like enterprise Java beans and their compositions in EJB.

The physical form of an assembly is a collection of DLL (dynamic link library) or EXE files (Fig. 5.13). These files are called modules, and contain code in Microsoft Intermediate Language (IL). The IL is a platform-independent set of

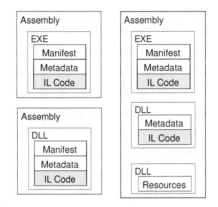

Fig. 5.13   .NET assemblies.

instructions into which all .NET-based languages (*e.g.* C# and Visual Basic) are compiled. In order to be executed, IL code is further compiled at run-time into machine code by the Just-in-Time (JIT) compiler.

An assembly must contain a manifest file and a metadata file for each module. It can also optionally contain resources (*e.g.* images). Specifically, manifest and metadata are files generated by the .NET-based language specific compiler. A manifest specifies the assembly's name, version, unique identifier, location and dependencies.[2] A metadata file lists the IL's classes, interfaces, methods and attributes.

Figure 5.14 shows a .NET assembly for ATM containing just one class ATM. The metadata shows the name of the class it is implementing (*ATM*), one of its methods (*LocateBank*) and the relevant parameters.

Just as a bundle is called a 'component' in OSGi literature, an assembly is called a 'component' in .NET literature. However, in terms of component models, there is no composition mechanism for assemblies; so assemblies are not components and .NET is not a component model, according to our definition of component models. Correspondingly, there is no notion of composite assemblies.

---

[2]This is similar to an OSGi bundle manifest (Section 5.3.2).

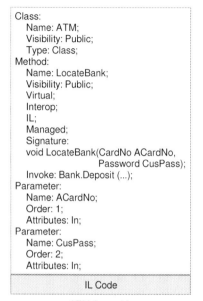

```
Class:
    Name: ATM;
    Visibility: Public;
    Type: Class;
Method:
    Name: LocateBank;
    Visibility: Public;
    Virtual;
    Interop;
    IL;
    Managed;
    Signature:
    void LocateBank(CardNo ACardNo,
                        Password CusPass);
    Invoke: Bank.Deposit (...);
Parameter:
    Name: ACardNo;
    Order: 1;
    Attributes: In;
Parameter:
    Name: CusPass;
    Order: 2;
    Attributes: In;
```

IL Code

ATM Assembly

Fig. 5.14　ATM assembly.

On the other hand, classes in assemblies are linked by method calls, and therefore they can be regarded as components composed by delegation. For this reason, we say that .NET is a framework that contains a component model with objects as components composed by delegation.

Figure 5.15 shows composition by delegation between objects in different .NET assemblies. In a banking system, an ATM object in the ATM assembly composes with a Bank object in the Bank assembly by invoking the latter's *Deposit* method.

Method calls in .NET assemblies are defined at design time. At runtime, the JIT compiler links the client calls to the required IL entry point. Specifically, the compilation of high-level code into IL produces machine-code stubs for every class method. Each stub calls into the JIT compiler, passing its own method address as parameter. At run-time, the JIT compiler retrieves the corresponding IL, compiles it into machine-code and replaces the stub in memory with the newly generated machine code. Figure 5.16 shows these interactions between .NET assemblies.

In terms of the idealised component life cycle, in the design phase, classes and their compositions are designed and coded (in a .NET language like C# or

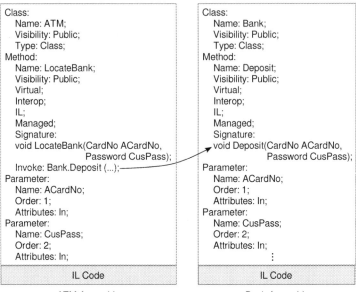

Fig. 5.15   .NET: objects in assemblies composed by delegation.

Visual Basic) using a suitable editor like *Microsoft Visual Studio*. These are compiled into .NET assemblies, which are deposited in the Microsoft Enterprise Library (MEL). Classes or assemblies cannot be retrieved from the repository for further composition; i.e. there is no assembler and hence no deployment phase. The MEL is thus a deposit-only repository, like an EJB container. This is depicted in Fig. 5.17. At run-time, client applications that use the assemblies in MEL invoke instances of .NET classes in these assemblies. The compositions of objects in these instances are as defined in the design phase.

Discussion and Further Reading

Confusingly, object-oriented frameworks are often called component models. This confusion arises partly because the term 'component model' is often used loosely in the sense that components can be any things that can be regarded as parts of a system, and their composition can be any code that glues them together.

Objects as components are particularly confusing since the only meaningful composition mechanism, i.e. delegation, is actually hard-coded in objects themselves. Objects are definitely not composable by explicit composition operators

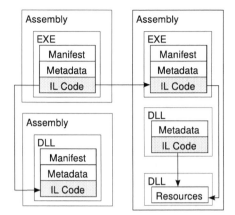

Fig. 5.16 .NET: interactions between assemblies.

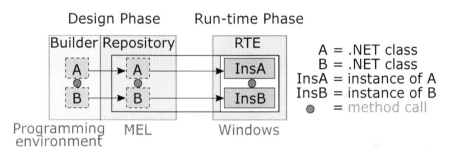

Fig. 5.17 .NET: component life cycle.

[Szyperski (2002a,b)]. To consider objects as components that are composed by (their own) code reinforces the confusion caused by loose usage of the term 'component model'.

Composing objects by delegation is definitely not an algebraic composition mechanism. Composing an object A with another object B does not yield another object; rather it yields a pair of objects $\langle A, B \rangle$. So the composition operation is a function of type $Object \times Object \rightarrow Object \times Object$, where $Object$ is the type of objects. An algebraic composition operation should be a function of type $Object \times Object \rightarrow Object$.

COM

COM (Component Object Model) [Box (1998)] has been superseded by .NET. We include it here for historical interest and for comparison with .NET and other object-oriented frameworks.

COM is very similar to a component model (such as POJOs and JavaBeans) with objects as components composed by delegation. It is also similar to a framework like EJB in that COM components (and their compositions) provide services that can be used by client applications.

COM components do not have to be objects, and can be defined in any language (with any internal state representation). Like an object, a COM component provides functionalities that can be called, but unlike an object, the functions of a COM component do not have to be methods of an object; they can be any executable binary that can be called via pointers (to the interface of the COM component). The interface of a COM component is a logical group of related functions, that together provide some well-defined capability. In other words, an interface is the contractual way for a COM component to expose its services.

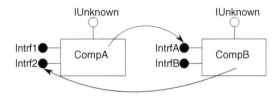

Fig. 5.18   COM: components and composition.

Figure 5.18 shows two COM components *CompA* and *CompB*. *CompA* implements the interfaces *Intrf1* and *Intrf2*, whereas *CompB* implements *IntrfA* and *IntrfB*.

Every COM component must implement the IUnknown interface, in order to control their own life cycle and to dynamically determine another component's capabilities. In order to ensure a a language-neutral architecture, COM interfaces are defined in the declarative Microsoft Interface Definition Language (MIDL) [Russell and Cohn (2012)]. An example is shown in Fig. 5.19, where the definition of a withdraw interface is illustrated. It is important to note that (i) in order to avoid

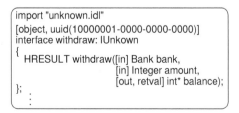

Fig. 5.19   Definition of the *withdraw* interface in MIDL.

naming clashing, each interface has an unique identifier (uuid); (ii) each argument of the *withdraw* method is preceded by a directional attribute [in] or [out].

Once defined, an MIDL interface can be compiled into several language source files. Then, with the help of a programming environment such as Visual Studio, a developer can implement the interfaces' behaviour and deposit the resulting component in the Windows registry.

COM components are composed by function calls via interface pointers (as can be seen in Fig. 5.18). In the design phase, a component declares which component interfaces it will connect to. The actual interface pointers are bound at run-time by the COM application server, as long as the referenced components are registered in the Windows registry.

Thus in terms of the idealised component life cycle, COM components and their compositions are designed and implemented in the design phase, and deposited in Windows Registry. This is illustrated in Fig. 5.20. There is no deployment phase since there is no further composition. At run-time, client applications make calls to COM components in the system via interface pointers.

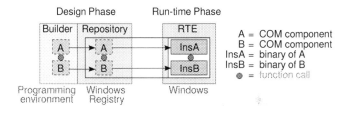

Fig. 5.20   COM: component life cycle.

It might be argued that in COM, composite components can be defined via *component containment* (Fig. 5.21(a)) and *component aggregation* (Fig. 5.21(b)). However, both techniques are used to define visibility aspects among COM components, not composition, as both outer and inner components can be deployed and distributed independently.

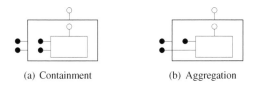

(a) Containment   (b) Aggregation

Fig. 5.21   COM: component containment and aggregation.

CCM

The CORBA Component Model (CCM) [BEA Systems *et al.* (1999); Siegel (2000); Marvie and Merle (2001); Bartlett (2001); OMG] is based on CORBA, the Common Object Request Broker Architecture, a standard defined by the Object Management Group (OMG), an international, open membership, not-for-profit technology standards consortium (http://www.omg.org/). CORBA (http://www.corba.org) is designed to facilitate the communication of systems that are deployed on diverse platforms.

In CCM a component is a CORBA meta-type that is an extension and specialisation of a CORBA Object [Natan (1995); Bolton (2001)], which is an object that can be invoked remotely in an object request broker architecture, via the use of Interface Definition Languages. A CCM component is hosted by a CCM container on a CCM platform such as OpenCCM (http://openccm.ow2.org/).

As shown in Fig. 5.22, a CCM component looks like an architectural unit which supports four kinds of ports:

- *facets*, which define the provided operation interfaces of the component;
- *receptacles*, which specify the required operation interfaces of the component;
- *event sources*, which publish or emit events of a specified type;
- *event sinks*, which consume events of a specified type.

Fig. 5.22   CCM: components.

CCM therefore looks like an ADL (see Chapter 6). However, CCM components are objects composed by method and event delegations in such a way that: (i) facets match receptacles; (ii) event sources match event sinks (Fig. 5.23). The

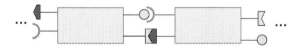

Fig. 5.23   CCM: composition.

composition of CCM components is specified by a Component Assembly Descriptor (an XML file).

In terms of the idealised component life cycle, CCM is similar to EJB, in that components are designed, composed and deposited in a container. In CCM, in the design phase, components are built using tools supplied by CCM providers such as OpenCCM, and deposited into a CCM container (Fig. 5.24). The CCM container

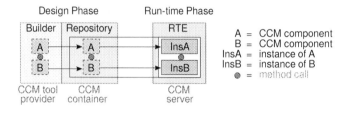

Fig. 5.24   CCM: component life cycle.

is hosted and managed by the chosen CCM platform. A component implementation (packaged into an assembly file) is deposited in a CCM server, which deploys and links its instances at run-time when invoked. CCM components are thus only composed in the design phase. Therefore there is no deployment phase. In the run-time phase, component instances are executed in the CCM container on the CCM server, when invoked by client applications.

KobrA

KobrA (Komponenten-basierte Anwendungsentwicklung)[3] [Atkinson *et al.* (2008, 2001)] is intended for modelling not just a single system but a family of related systems.[4]

A KobrA component (Komponent) is a UML component as defined in UML 1.x [Cheesman and Daniels (2001)], not UML 2.x (see Section 6.3). It is described by a set of textual and UML models at two distinct levels of abstraction referred to as *Komponent specification* (top, Fig. 5.25) and *Komponent realisation* level (bottom, Fig. 5.25).

At specification level, the external visible proprieties of a component are defined by four categories of models. They are *structural* model (UML class diagram), *behavioural* model (UML statechart diagram), *functional model* (textual model) and *decision* model (textual model). The functional model describes in words the expected behaviour of the component. The decision model describes the conditions under which the component will be selected to be in a particular system. It therefore represents variability in the family of systems.

---

[3] Component-based application development.
[4] Koala (Section 6.5) also models product families.

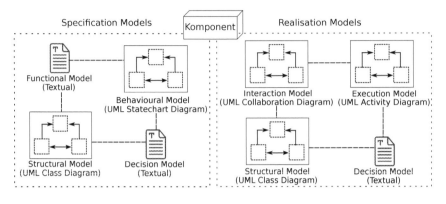

Fig. 5.25   KobrA component (adapted from [Atkinson *et al.* (2000)]).

Similarly, at realisation level the private design of a component is described by four categories of models: *interaction* model (UML collaboration diagram), *structural* model (UML class diagram), *execution* model (UML activity diagram) and *decision* model (textual model).

As UML models are translated and implemented in an object-oriented programming language, KobrA components are implemented as objects in an object-oriented programming language, composed by direct method calls.

In terms of the idealised component life cycle, in the design phase, KobrA models for components are defined using a UML visual builder tool as the builder, and stored as files in the tool's file system (Fig. 5.26). To build a particular system,

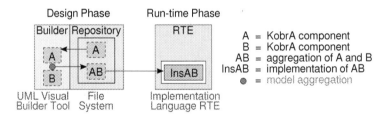

Fig. 5.26   KobrA: component life cycle.

these models are aggregated into a model for the system according to the variability defined in the decision models. In this process, components are composed by method calls. There is no deployment phase, since the system has been completely modelled in the design phase. Then the modelled system has to be implemented in a chosen object-oriented programming language. It is then executed in the run-time environment of that language.

Enterprise JavaBeans

In EJB, composition of EJBs is realised at run-time by the container, which either injects the dependencies between beans [Prasanna (2009)], or uses the Java Naming and Directory Interface (JNDI) [Lee and Seligman (2000)] syntax to find the bean instances involved.

Although some work has been done, *e.g.* [Choi *et al.* (2002); Goebel and Nestler (2004)], it is not clear how a composite EJB can be defined or used in further compositions.

Chapter 6

Component Models with Architectural Units as Components

In this chapter, we describe component models where components are architectural units. These models are defined by *architecture description languages*
(ADLs) [Clements (1996); Medvidovic and Taylor (2000); Mishra and Dutt
(2011)]. The archetypal example is Acme (Section 6.1).

As its name suggests, an ADL defines a *software architecture* [Perry and Wolf
(1992); Shaw and Garlan (1996); Taylor *et al.* (2009); Bass *et al.* (2012)], i.e.
the visible parts of a software system and their inter-relationships. Each part of
a software architecture is called an *architectural unit*; it is a unit of behaviour
and/or data. Architectural units have ports for input and output, and are linked (via
their ports) by connectors that define their inter-relationships. A connector can
convey data as well as control. Architectural units collaborate and communicate
via connectors, by invoking one another's behaviour through indirect message
passing, and passing data to one another. The behaviour of the whole system
starts with a *main* method either in one of the architectural units or in a client
application that invokes one of the architectural units.

As in Chapter 5, for each component model we describe, we will also analyse
the component life cycle in that model, and compare it to the idealised component
life cycle (Section 1.1), in order to see how well the component model supports
the latter.

6.1 Acme

Acme [Aldrich *et al.* (2004); Schmerl and Garlan (2004); Garlan *et al.* (2000,
2010); Acme] in its entirety is more than an ADL (see Discussion and Further
Reading). It is really a meta model for ADLs, and as such its foundations and
underlying concepts underpin all ADLs. Here we focus on Acme's core elements
for modelling architectures: *components*, *connectors*, *ports* and *systems* (Fig. 6.1).

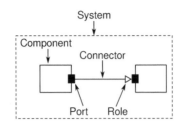

Fig. 6.1   Acme elements.

In Acme, *components* are the primary units of computation and data of a system. A component may have multiple interfaces (*ports*), which identify the points of interaction between the component and its environment. An interface can be as simple as a procedure signature, or as complicated as a collection of procedure calls that must be invoked in certain specific orders.

Figure 6.2 shows examples of Acme components. The *ATM* component receives requests (via its *receiveReq* port) from the bank customers and pass them (via its *sendReq* port) on to the bank consortium component *BC* (via its *receiveOp* port), which in turn will pass on the requests (via its *sendOp* port) to the customers' bank branches.

Component ATM = { Port receiveReq, Port sendReq }
Component BC = { Port receiveOp, Port sendOp }

Fig. 6.2   Acme: components.

Components in Acme are composed by *connectors* between them. Connectors mediate communication and coordination among components. Examples include simple forms of interaction, such as pipe, procedure call, and event broadcast. However, connectors can also represent more complex interactions, such as a client-server protocol or a SQL link between a database and an application.

Connectors have interfaces defined by a set of *roles*. Each role defines a participant of the interaction. For instance, a simple RPC connector has a caller and a callee roles, whereas a pipe connector has a writer and a reader roles. On the other hand, connectors may have more than two roles. For example, an event-broadcaster connector might have one source role and an arbitrary number of event-receiver roles.

Components are composed by binding their ports to the connectors' roles. This binding is specified in *attachments*. Figure 6.3 shows a connector *ConnA* that composes the *ATM* and *BC* components (Fig. 6.2). *ConnA* has two roles: request

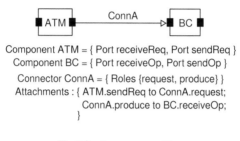

```
Component ATM = { Port receiveReq, Port sendReq }
Component BC = { Port receiveOp, Port sendOp }
Connector ConnA = { Roles {request, produce} }
Attachments : { ATM.sendReq to ConnA.request;
                ConnA.produce to BC.receiveOp;
              }
```

Fig. 6.3   Acme: composition.

and produce, which are respectively bound to the *ATM*'s *sendReq* port and *BC*'s *receiveOp* port, as specified in the attachments.

In Acme, a *system* represents an application's architecture as a graph in which nodes denote components and lines denote connectors attached to components' ports. Both elements may represent subsystems that have their own internal architectures.

Figure 6.4 depicts a simple bank system (*BankSys*) and its architecture in Acme. The *ATM*, the bank consortium component (*BC*) and the connector (*ConnA*) are as defined in Fig. 6.3. According to the operation received on the *receiveOp* port, the component *BC* dispatches the task to either the *Bank1* or *Bank2* component via the connectors *ConnB* and *ConnC* respectively. The architecture of this system is defined by listing a set of attachments that bind components' ports to connectors' roles.

In terms of the idealised component life-cycle, in Acme (and all Acme-like ADLs), in the design phase the architecture of the system is modelled, in terms of (models of) components and connectors (Fig. 6.5). This can be done using the AcmeStudio tool [AcmeStudio]. Since an Acme architecture is only a model, the components are not coded, so there is no repository, and therefore no deployment phase. Acme models of components and architectures have to be implemented in a chosen programming language, e.g. Java. At run-time, the implemented system is executed in the run-time environment of that programming language.

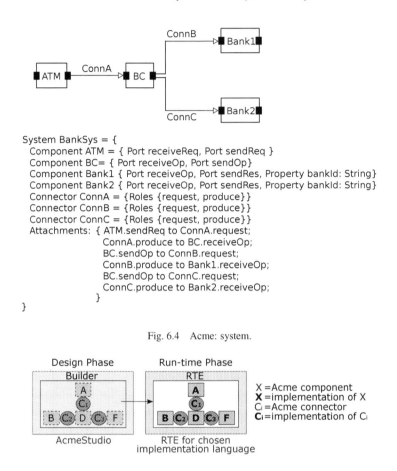

Fig. 6.4   Acme: system.

Fig. 6.5   Acme: component life cycle.

6.2   ArchJava

ArchJava [Aldrich *et al.* (2002, 2004)] is an ADL that is based on the Acme model. However, unlike Acme, which only defines models, ArchJava is actually a programming language for defining components and architectures. In fact, ArchJava is an extension of Java in which an architectural unit (with ports) can be defined as a special public class called *component* class. A component class in ArchJava is denoted by the *component* keyword. It can have ports, denoted by the *port* keyword, that specify services *required* and *provided* by the component. As architectural units, ArchJava components can be composed via their ports into an architecture. Such an architecture, like in Acme, can have multiple subsystems and hence multiple levels of composition.

An ArchJava component is an instance of a component class. It is a special kind of object that communicates with other components in a structured manner. A component can only communicate with other components at the same level in the architecture through its ports. Direct method calls between components are not allowed. Instead, ports declare methods. These methods are denoted by the keywords: *requires*, *provides* and *broadcasts*. A provided method is implemented by the component and can be called by other components connected to this port. A required method is provided by some other component connected to this port. A component can invoke a required method by sending a message to the port (of a provider component) that defines the required method. Broadcast methods are just like required methods, except that they can be connected to any number of ports (that define them) and must return *void*.[1]

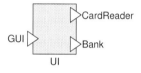

Fig. 6.6   An architectural unit.

Figure 6.6 shows an architectural unit *UI* that is a user interface component. *U I* provides a bank's customers with an interface to an ATM. It has a port *GUI* which provides a service (graphical user interface) to bank customers, a port *CardReader* which requires services (customer inputs) from a card reader, and another port called *Bank* which requires services (requested by the customer) from the bank.

This architectural unit can be defined as the ArchJava component in Fig. 6.7.[2] The *GUI* port defines a provided service *display* for displaying a screen to the customer. The *Bank* port requires the usual *deposit*, *withdraw* and *balance* services that customers can request. The *CardReader* port requires a service *readAccountNo* to read the customer's account number.

ArchJava components can be composed into a composite component by connecting (compatible) ports of different components. For example, the *UI* component in Figs. 6.6 and 6.7 can be composed with a *CardReader* component and a *Bank* component into a composite component *ATM* as shown in Fig. 6.8. The ArchJava code for *ATM* is shown in Fig. 6.9. A connection between two ports is made by using the *connect* keyword followed by the names of the two ports

---

[1] For simplicity we do not consider broadcast methods.

[2] ArchJava does not formally define a graphical notation, so we give only code for the component.

```
public component class UI{
    public port GUI{
        provides void display();
    }
    public port Bank{
        requires void deposit(String accno, Double amount);
        requires void withdraw(String accno, Double amount);
        requires Double balance(String accno);
    }
    public port CardReader{
        requires String readAccNo();
    }
}
```

Fig. 6.7   ArchJava: component.

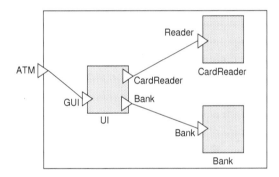

Fig. 6.8   ArchJava: composition.

being connected. In addition, ports of the constituent components of a composite component can be forwarded to become ports of the composite component. Ports that are not forwarded to the composite will be hidden inside the composite. Port forwarding is specified by the keyword *glue*.

In the example, the composite component *ATM* is defined as a component class called *ATMSystem*. The sub-components *UI* and *CardReader* are composed through a connection between a pair of ports which are *CardReader* and *Reader*. The port *GUI* of sub-component *UI* is forwarded to become port *ATM* of the composite component.

A system built in ArchJava is a composite component, like *ATMSystem* in Fig. 6.9. Such a component is the top-level component of the system and so it has the *main* method of the system.

```
public component class ATMSystem{
    public port ATM{
        provides void start();
    }
    // Define sub-components
    private UI gui = new UI();
    private Bank bank = new Bank();
    private CardReader cardReader = new CarReader();

    // Compose sub-components
    connect gui.CardReader, cardReader.Reader;
    connect gui.Bank, bank.Bank;
    glue this.ATM, gui.GUI;
}
```

Fig. 6.9   ArchJava: composite component.

In terms of the idealised component life cycle, ArchJava has the same component life cycle as Acme. In ArchJava, in the design phase, the system and all the

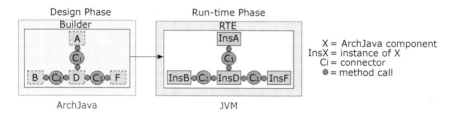

Fig. 6.10   ArchJava: component life cycle.

components are designed, like in Acme. However, unlike Acme, code is written for all the components and their composition (connections). This is illustrated in Fig. 6.10, which shows explicitly that there are no direct method calls between the components, only indirect ones via ports (connections). No components are deposited in a repository, so there is no repository and therefore there is no deployment phase. The code for the whole system created in the design phase is compiled and executed in the JVM in the run-time phase, where components are objects that are instances of ArchJava classes defined in the design phase.

6.3   UML

The definition of components (and architectures) in UML (the Unified Modeling Language) has changed over time (see Discussion and Further Reading). Initially UML considered components only as implementation artefacts, so did not define an ADL for modelling components and architectures like Acme (Section 6.1). However, starting with UML 2.0, UML 2.x provides such an ADL.

UML 2.0 introduced *structured classifiers*, which are classifiers that can be decomposed internally. A component is a structured classifier, and as such is a structured class which is a containment of its (sub)parts, i.e. it has containment links to all its (sub)parts. With these components and with connectors for components and their (sub)parts, UML 2.0 and its successors UML 2.x provide architecture modelling concepts along the lines of Acme.

A component in a UML 2.x architecture is a modular unit of the system, with well-defined interfaces, that is replaceable within its environment by an equivalent unit, in particular one that is a decomposition of the component. A UML 2.x component is represented as a rectangle with either the stereotype ⟨⟨*component*⟩⟩, or with a visual stereotype (defined in UML 1.x) which is a component icon in the upper right corner of the rectangle, as shown in Fig. 6.11. A UML 2.x component

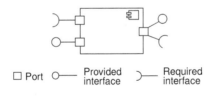

Fig. 6.11   UML 2.x: components.

specifies the services that it can provide or require through its interfaces, grouped into ports. Graphically, a port is represented as a square, a provided interface as a lollipop, and a required interface as a socket. Semantically, a port defines an interaction point between a component and its environment, or between a component and a particular part of its internal structure (its decomposition) actually providing or requiring the service exposed by an interface. A port that has both provided and required interfaces is called *bidirectional*. Figure 6.11 contains such a port.

Since in UML 2.x a component is a containment of its internal decomposition, components are always composed inside a higher-level component that is the composite component. They are composed by wiring their compatible required and provided interfaces together. As depicted in Fig. 6.12, this can be done by means of two types of UML connectors: *assembly connectors* and *delegation connectors*. An assembly connector connects matching ports in terms of their provided

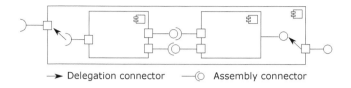

——► Delegation connector   ——○ Assembly connector

Fig. 6.12   UML 2.x: composition.

and required services. It also provides a containment link from the higher level component to its constituent parts. A delegation connector provides the wiring from higher level provided interfaces to lower level ones, and from lower level required interfaces to higher level ones.[3] Delegation connectors can be used to model the hierarchical decomposition of behaviour, where services provided by a component may ultimately be realized by a sub-component that is nested multiple levels deep within it.

Figure 6.13 shows an example of a bank system with a UML 2.x architecture. The bank system consists of a consortium of banks. The consortium offers an ATM which allows customers of the banks in the consortium to access their

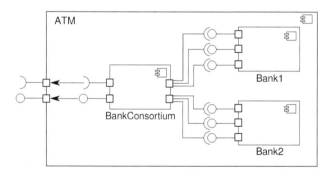

Fig. 6.13   UML 2.x: a bank system.

accounts at their own banks. The components, along with their required and provided services, forming the bank system are shown in Fig. 6.14. The component *ATM* provides a *GetCardNo* service, whereas it requires a *CheckBankID* interface. The latter is provided by the component *BankConsortium*, which in turn requires *GetCardNo* to identify the customer, along with the operations *Withdraw*, *Deposit* and *CheckBalance*. The implementation of these operations is provided by the components *Bank1* and *Bank2*.

---

[3]A delegation corresponds to Acme's *rep-map* concept.

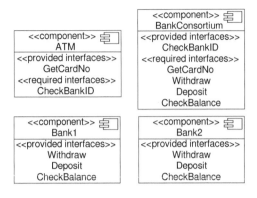

Fig. 6.14   UML 2.x: components of a bank system.

In UML 2.x, parts of a system can be specified directly by behaviour, rather than classes. For instance, if a class's behaviour is delegated to its parts, then the latter can be specified by using UML's behavioural diagrams such as state charts and activity charts.

Finally, in terms of the idealised component life cycle, UML 2.x has a similar component life cycle to Acme and ArchJava. In the design phase, the system and its components are designed together in a visual builder tool such as Eclipse Papyrus[4] (Fig. 6.15). This design represents a (structured) class diagram in which all

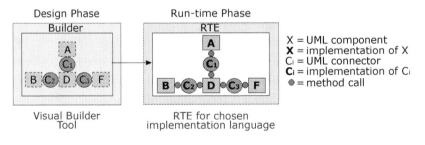

Fig. 6.15   UML 2.x: component life cycle.

entities are represented as classes. In particular, components are just (structured) class diagrams. Like in Acme, no components are implemented at this stage, and therefore there is no repository, and there is no deployment phase. This entire design has to be implemented (somehow) in a chosen programming language, and executed in the run-time phase in the run-time environment of that programming

---

[4]https://eclipse.org/papyrus/

language. As UML is an object-oriented methodology, all the classes in the design are implemented as objects, like in ArchJava. Therefore all the objects in the implementation, including components (and their parts, e.g. ports) and connectors are linked by method calls, again like in ArchJava.

6.4 ProCom

Acme, ArchJava and UML 2.x are generic rather than domain-specific. By contrast, ProCom [Sentilles *et al.* (2008); Vulgarakis *et al.* (2009)] is an example of a domain-specific component model: it is intended for the domain of real-time systems.

ProCom is a two-layered component model: ProSys for the system layer and ProSave for the subsystem layer. At the system layer, ProSys components are *subsystems*, or rather, active, distributed components with typed input and output *message ports* (Fig. 6.16). They are composed via explicit (asynchronous)

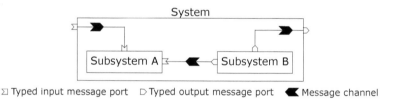

Fig. 6.16   ProSys: components and composition.

message channels. The types of messages received and sent by a subsystem are specified by its message ports.

At the subsystem layer, ProSys components are internally modelled by ProSave components. A ProSave component is a passive unit of functionality, designed to encapsulate low-level tasks, e.g. control loops. ProSave distinguishes between data and control flow. Indeed, it uses a pipe-and-filter architectural style where data flows to *data ports* and control to *trigger ports*. As depicted in Fig. 6.17, a ProSave component exposes its functionality via services, each consisting of: (i) an input group of ports, which contains the activation trigger and required data; (ii) an output group of ports, which makes available the data produced. The behaviour of a *primitive* ProSave component is realised by code, whereas the behaviour of a *composite* ProSave component is realised by interconnected sub-components. For primitive components, in addition to an initialiser function, each service is implemented by a single non-suspending C function. Figure 6.17 shows a primitive ProSave component S_1 and the corresponding C header file.

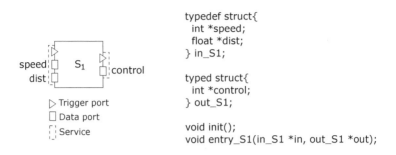

```
typedef struct{
    int *speed;
    float *dist;
} in_S1;

typed struct{
    int *control;
} out_S1;

void init();
void entry_S1(in_S1 *in, out_S1 *out);
```

Fig. 6.17   ProSave: a primitive component and its C header file [Sentilles *et al.* (2008)].

ProSave components are composed by *connections* and *connectors*. A connection is a directed edge which connects two matching ports (output data port to input data port of compatible types and output trigger port to input trigger port). Connectors are constructs that provide further regulation over data and control flow. The set of connectors in ProSave includes connectors for forking and joining data or trigger connections: *data fork*, *data or*, *control fork*, *control join*, *control or*; or selecting dynamically a path of the control flow depending on a condition: *control selection*. Figure 6.18 shows an example of a Prosave composite component. Its internal structure is composed of three components (C_1, C_2, C_3) composed by a *control fork* and a *data fork* connectors.

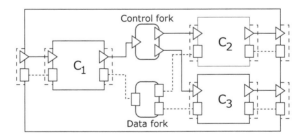

Fig. 6.18   ProSave: a composite component.

In order to integrate the system and sub-system levels, ProCom includes two further ProSave connectors: (i) one that maps message-passing to pipe-and-filter (and vice-versa); (ii) a clock that specifies periodic activation of ProSave components.

Finally, in terms of the idealised component life cycle, in the design phase in ProCom, a complete ProSave system is designed and built in the PRIDE tool, from ProSave components that have been designed and built for the system, also using PRIDE, and deposited in the tool's repository (Fig. 6.19). Thus in design phase, both ProSave components and the complete ProSys system are fully coded. There is no deployment phase. At run-time, the binary of the system is executed using the implementation language run-time environment (C/C++).

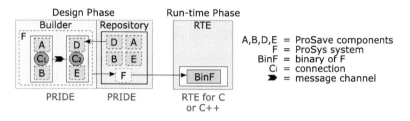

Fig. 6.19 ProCom: component life cycle.

6.5 Koala

Like ProCom, Koala (C[K]omponent Organizer And Linking Assistant) [van Ommering *et al.* (2000); van Ommering and Bosch (2002)], developed by Philips, is another component model designed for a specific domain: consumer electronics. Unlike ProCom, however, Koala is designed to describe not just a single system but a family of systems, i.e. a product line [Pohl *et al.* (2005); Clements and Northrop (2015)] of consumer electronic products. Components and composition in Koala are defined accordingly.

A Koala component is a unit of design and implementation which interacts with its environment (other components) via interfaces. A Koala component implements a function, and calls functions defined in other components. Figure 6.20 shows a Koala component with interfaces represented as squares containing a triangle. In an interface, triangle tip orientation specifies the direction of a function

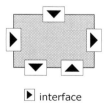

Fig. 6.20 Koala: components.

call and hence the interface type. A tip pointing inside a component specifies a *provided interface*, as the function is implemented within the component; whereas a tip pointing outside a component identifies a *required interface*.

Interfaces are described, and stored in a global repository, using a simple Interface Description Language (IDL) in which function prototypes are listed in C syntax. For instance, the following is the implementation of a VolumeControl interface in IDL.

```
interface VolumeControl{
    void setVolume(int v);
    int  getVolume(void);
    int a_constant = 3;
    int a_parameter;
}
```

Like interfaces, components are described, and stored in a global repository, using a Component Description Language (CDL), in which provided and required interfaces are listed. For instance, the following example is an Amplifier component.

```
Component Amplifier{
    provides VolumeControl vol;
    requires VolumeStabilizer stb;
}
```

In terms of design at architectural level, a component consists of a set of C header files[5] contained in a single directory. Files within a directory can be freely imported and used, but they can not have external references. In terms of implementation, a Koala component also needs C code to be written for the function it implements.

Koala components are composed by connecting their interfaces. As depicted in Fig. 6.21, required and provided interfaces are connected following two simple composition rules: (i) a required interface must be bound to exactly one provided interface; (ii) a provided interface can be bound with zero or more required interfaces.

A direct connection among interfaces is not always sufficient, as it assumes that components are completely tuned and do not change during their evolution. For this reason, interfaces are connected through an interface-less component called *module* (**m** in Fig. 6.21). A Koala module represents the connection point

---

[5] Although Koala is not bound to the C programming language, all existing components are written in C and the tool only works for C files.

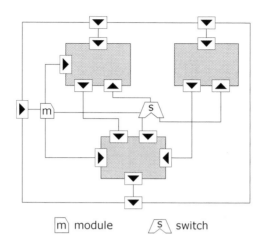

m module   s switch

Fig. 6.21   Koala: composition.

between architectural and realization levels; this implies that Koala component composition amounts to constructing modules. Indeed, a module implements all the functions of all the bound provided interfaces, while it has access to any bound required interfaces.

Figure 6.22 depicts an example of a stabilised amplifier built in Koala. The system contains two sub-components *Amplifier* and *Volume Stabiliser*. Each component contains a module which implements the provided interfaces. Therefore a module *a_impl* implements the interface *VolumeControl* exposed by *Amplifier*. Similarly, the module *s_impl* realises the methods exposed by the interface *VolumeStabiliser* exposed by the component *Volume Stabiliser*. Finally, the module *stbAmpVol_impl* within the component *Stabilised_Amplifier* connects the provided interface *StabilisedAmplifiedVolume* with the interface *VolumeControl* exposed by the component *Amplifier*, and realises the connection between the latter with *Volume Stabiliser*.

As Koala has been designed as a component model for building families of related products, a diversity mechanism is needed. A component may change its internal structure (via cpp directives) according to parameters received from a special, yet standard, kind of required interface called diversity interface. At architectural level, switches (**s** in Fig. 6.21) use parameters to re-route connections between interfaces. Koala can automatically remove unreachable components and implementation code therein.

In terms of the idealised component life cycle, in the design phase, Koala components (definition files) are built in the Koala programming environment and

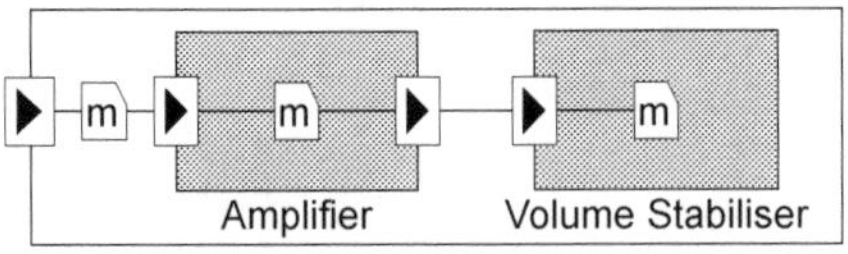

Stabilised Amplifier

```
Component Amplifier{
provides VolumeControl vol;
requires VolumeStabiliser stb;
contains module a_impl present;
connects vol = a_impl;
         a_impl = stb;


}

Component Volume_Stabiliser{
provides VolumeStabiliser stb;
contains module s_impl present;
connects stb = s_impl;
}
Component Stabilised_Amplifier{
provides StabilisedAmplifiedVolume stbAmpVol;
contains component Amplifier amp;
contains component Volume_Stabiliser stb;
contains module stbAmpVol_impl present;
connects vst = stbAmpVol_impl;
connects amp.stb = stb.stb;
}
```

Fig. 6.22   Koala: example of a system.

deposited in the file system *KoalaModel Workspace* (Fig. 6.23). These components are retrieved from the repository and composed into a system (a definition file), and also deposited in the *WorkSpace*. The definition files for the system and the components are compiled (by the Koala compiler) into C header files. To fully implement the components and the system, C files are written for them, and compiled into binary C code. The system is fully designed and codes at this stage. There is therefore no further composition, and no deployment phase. At run-time, the binary code of the system is executed in the run-time environment of C.

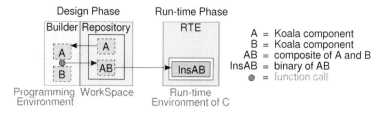

Fig. 6.23   Koala: component life cycle.

6.6   FRACTAL

As we saw in Section 5.3, there are object-oriented frameworks, e.g. OSGi, that provide building blocks, e.g. bundles, built from, and therefore larger than, objects. These building blocks are not always components for lack of composition, e.g. OSGi bundles do not compose, and as a result, from the point of view of component models, these frameworks still only contain objects as components. Another object-oriented framework, called FRACTAL, also has objects as components, but in addition it provides an ADL for structuring groups of objects into architectural units.

The key objective of FRACTAL [Bruneton *et al.* (2006)] is to support designing and implementing reconfigurable (distributed) object-oriented systems in a modular manner. To this end, FRACTAL components support introspection, in order that its internal features can be identified and reconfigured.

FRACTAL defines components in a similar manner to UML 2.x, i.e. as software units that can be decomposed internally. A FRACTAL component (Fig. 6.24) consists of a *membrane*, which supports interfaces to introspect and reconfigure its internal features, and a *content*, which consists of a finite set of sub-components.

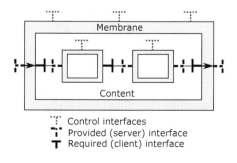

Fig. 6.24   FRACTAL: components.

A component has *provided* and *required* interfaces (for provided and required services), as well as *control* interfaces in its membrane.

FRACTAL does not enforce a pre-determined set of controllers in components' membranes. However, it identifies the controllers required for specific levels of control (or reflection capabilities) a developer may want to achieve for a component. At the lowest level of control, a FRACTAL component is comparable to a POJO with no introspection and interception capabilities.

At the next level of control, a FRACTAL component provides a Component interface, which is similar to the IUnknown interface in COM (see section 5.3.3), and enables an elementary means for introspecting the internal structure of a component. It is at this level and above that FRACTAL provides an ADL (using XML for structuring components).

At higher levels of control, a FRACTAL component enables additional introspection and interception capabilities. FRACTAL provides several examples of controller interfaces, which can be combined and extended to yield components with different reflective features. They are *attribute controller*, *binding controller*, *content controller* and *life-cycle controller*.

In FRACTAL ADL, components can be *primitive* or *composite*, and they are composed by binding their interfaces to one another. A primitive component has no sub-components, and is implemented by a class. It can be defined by specifying the interfaces it provides, the interfaces it requires, and the class that implements it. In the ATM system in Fig. 6.25, the components *CardReader*, *ATMEngine*, *BankA* and *BankB* are all primitive components.

A composite component has sub-components, and is defined by specifying its sub-components, like in UML 2.x, and the interface bindings between these sub-components. The ATM system in Fig. 6.25 is a composite component, with sub-components *CardReader*, *ATMEngine*, *BankA* and *BankB*.

A binding can be either *primitive* if the bound interfaces are in the same address space, or *composite* if the bound interfaces span different address spaces. While a primitive binding can be readily implemented via pointer or direct language references (*i.e.* method calls), a composite one is embodied in a binding object which itself takes the form of a FRACTAL component, whose role is to mediate communication between the bound components. Moreover, FRACTAL allows a component to be *shared* among several components; this enables sharing the state of a component.

Figure 6.25 illustrates component composition in FRACTAL. It shows an example of a simplified ATM system realised in FRACTAL as a composite component with sub-components *CardReader*, *ATMEngine*, *BankA* and *BankB*. The system requires two services (*CardNo* and *Operation*) in order to submit the required operation (*e.g.* show balance) to the right bank component.

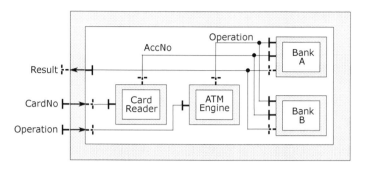

Fig. 6.25 FRACTAL: ATM system.

Finally, in terms of the idealised component lifecycle, one would expect FRACTAL to have a similar component life cycle to an ADL like ArchJava. However, this is not the case, because whereas an ADL produces only a design, and no code, in the design phase, the ADL in FRACTAL is used to structure and compose (configure) code for the whole system in the design phase. In the design phase, FRACTAL components are designed and the architecture of the complete system is constructed by composing components, via their interface bindings. This is illustrated in Fig. 6.26. FRACTAL components and the complete system are built in the

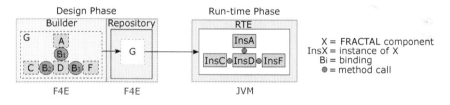

Fig. 6.26 FRACTAL: component life cycle.

FRACTAL for Eclipse (F4E) IDE,[6] which also serves as a deposit-only repository for the system. There is no assembler or deployment phase. In the Java implementation of FRACTAL, called JULIA,[7] in the run-time phase, the complete FRACTAL system built in the design phase is executed as an object-oriented system on a Java Virtual Machine (JVM).

---

[6]http://fractal.ow2.org/f4e/
[7]http://fractal.ow2.org/java.html For other implementations, see http://fractal.ow2.org/.

Discussion and Further Reading

Component models with architectural units as components are the most widely used category of component models in practice. Clearly it is not possible to cover them all here. The ones we have covered provide a good representation of the category. Many of the ones we have not covered are becoming obsolete. In this section, we will briefly discuss some of these, for historical interest and for comparison with similar models that we have covered in this chapter. We will also further discuss the latter models, as usual.

Acme, ArchJava and UML 2.x are examples of *first-generation* ADLs, which are aimed at designing complete systems from scratch, identifying and creating components for the system under construction. Typically these ADLs do not consider building components for a repository or retrieving them from a repository. Rather they are used to construct the complete system, either as a model, as in Acme and UML 2.x, or in a programming language, as in ArchJava. The system then has to be either implemented, as in Acme and UML 2.x, or executed as is in the programming language run-time, as in ArchJava.

ProCom, Koala and FRACTAL are examples of *second-generation* ADLs. These make use of a repository, to store components implemented (in a chosen programming language) for the system and possibly for the domain, and the complete design of the system in the ADL using these components. The design of the system is then compiled and executed in the run-time of the implementation language.

SCA

Service Component Architecture (SCA) [SCA-IBM] is a software technology designed to provide a model for composing applications that follow service-oriented architecture (SOA) [Erl (2005)] principles. The technology, created by major software vendors, including IBM, Oracle and TIBCO, encompasses a wide range of disparate technologies and as such is defined in various independent specifications in order to maintain programming language and application environment neutrality. Here we give a brief account of the underlying component model, which is an ADL like Acme.

Whatever technology is used, every component contains a common set of abstractions, including *services*, *references*, *properties*, and *bindings*, to specify its behaviour and its interactions with the outside world. Figure 6.27 depicts an SCA component. A component typically implements some business logic, exposed as one or more services. How services are described depends on the technology

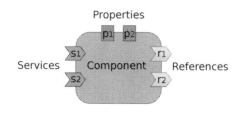

Fig. 6.27   SCA: component.

that is used to implement the component. A Java component, for example, might describe its services using ordinary Java interfaces, while a component implemented in BPEL [OASIS (2007)] would likely describe its services using the *Web Service Description Language* (WSDL) [WSDL]. Along with providing services to its own clients, a component might also rely on services provided by other components in its domain or by software outside its domain. To describe this, a component can use references to indicate the services it relies on.

A composite in SCA is depicted in Fig. 6.28: components are composed by wiring matching services and references together. Services and references let a

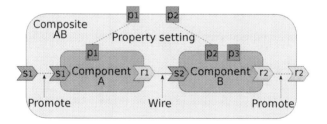

Fig. 6.28   SCA: composition.

component communicate with other software, including other components. By design, however, they say nothing about how that communication happens. Specifying this is the job of *bindings*. Each binding defines a particular protocol that can be used to communicate with this service or reference. A single service or reference can have multiple bindings, allowing different remote software to communicate with it in different ways. SCA allows each *remotable* service and each reference to specify the protocols it supports using bindings. For example, to be accessible via SOAP over HTTP, an SCA service uses the Web Services binding, while to be accessible via a queued messaging protocol it uses the Java Message Service (JMS) binding. Similarly, the EJB session bean binding allows access to session beans using the Internet Inter-ORB Protocol (IIOP).

A composite is a logical construct: its components can run in a single process on a single computer or be distributed across multiple processes on multiple computers. The components making up each composite might all use the same technology, or they might be built using different technologies. An SCA composite is typically described in an associated configuration file, the name of which ends in *.composite*. This file uses an XML-based format called *Service Component Definition Language* to describe components forming the composite and their relationships.

Components and composites are the fundamental elements of every SCA application. Both are contained within a larger construct called *domain*. Domains are an important concept in SCA. Even though SCA allows creating distributed applications, it does not fully define how components on different machines should interact. As a result, the communication among these components will be implemented differently by different products. Therefore, each domain delimits the area related to each product, or more generally related to a single vendor (*e.g.* IBM). A domain can contain one or more composites, each of which has components implemented in one or more processes running on one or more machines.

In terms of the idealised component life cycle, in SCA, components, composites and systems are all designed and implemented in the design phase (Fig. 6.29), in a chosen programming language (and using a chosen technology), using an

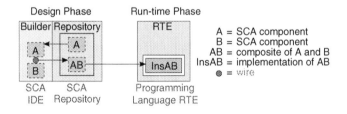

Fig. 6.29   SCA: component life cycle.

SCA IDE as the builder. Services and references are connected by wire to compose components into composites and systems. Components and composites can be stored in the repository of the SCA tool, and used to construct systems, also using the builder of the SCA IDE. There is no deployment phase since systems are completely designed and implemented in the design phase. In the run-time phase, a complete system is executed in the run-time environment of the chosen programming language (using the chosen technology).

SOFA

SOFA (SOFtware Appliances) is similar to FRACTAL in the way it defines components and their composition. Like a FRACTAL component, a SOFA component has a control interface, a provided interface, a required interface, and a content (sub-components) (Fig. 6.30). In SOFA 2 [Bures *et al.* (2006)] a component is

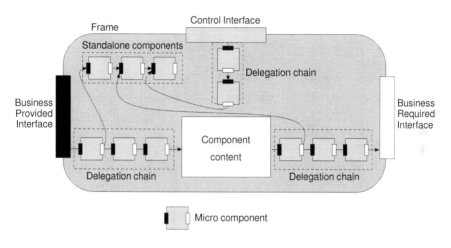

Fig. 6.30   SOFA: component.

described by its frame and architecture. The former provides a black-box view of the component defining its required and provided interfaces (called business provided and required interfaces); the latter defines the frame implementation by specifying the component's sub-components and their interconnections, i.e. the component content, at the first level of nesting.

Like in FRACTAL, SOFA components are composed by binding their interfaces together. All bindings are provided by connectors, which are first-class entities. SOFA 2 distinguishes between design and runtime connectors. Design connectors specify the communication style (procedure call, messaging, streaming, or blackboard), whereas runtime connectors implement them.

Similar to FRACTAL, SOFA 2 facilitates dynamic reconfiguration. However, in order to prevent uncontrolled modifications of an architecture, SOFA 2 only allows a special case of dynamic reconfiguration called *dynamic update* [Hnětynka and Plášil (2006)]: the replacement of a component with another one having compatible interfaces. A component's runtime structure is realised by a modular and extensible control part. The general idea of controller stems from FRACTAL (see Section 6.6). The control part of a component is modelled as a set of micro-components composed together. The micro-component model is a very minimalist one – it is flat (no nested micro-components) featuring no connectors and no distribution. Additionally, to avoid recursion, a micro-component does not have any extensible or structured parts. In principle a micro-controller is just a class implementing a specified interface.

On top of micro-components, SOFA defines aspect-consistent extensions of the control part. An aspect comprises a definition of micro-components and a micro-component instantiation patterns. By applying a number of aspects, a control part with the desired functionality is obtained. The aspects to be applied are specified at configuration time (called deployment time in SOFA). There is a core aspect in SOFA 2, which is present in all controllers. This core aspect introduces the control interfaces of a life-cycle controller (starting/stopping/updating) and a binding controller (adding/removing connections among components) and provides the basic functionality of these controllers.

The runtime environment of a SOFA 2 system resides on a distributed runtime environment called SOFAnodes [Sobr and Tuma (2005)]. A SOFAnode contains a repository of components and a number of deployment docks. A deployment dock is a component container (JVM + SOFA runtime), which provides runtime functionality for executing components. An application can span several deployment docks within one SOFAnode.

A SOFAnode can execute component applications by obtaining the components from the repository, instantiating and interconnecting them as described in the system's architecture. Installing, uninstalling and upgrading a component application or its part is done simply by populating the repository of the SOFAnode. Thus, the repository is used throughout the whole application life-cycle as the central source of component description as well as a code base.

In terms of the idealised component life cycle, SOFA has the same component life cycle as FRACTAL, unsurprisingly. Like in FRACTAL, in the design phase, components are designed and the architecture of the complete system is constructed by composing components, via their interface bindings, using a SOFA IDE, which provides a deposit-only repository for the system. This is illustrated in Fig. 6.31. There is no assembler or deployment phase (in the sense of the idealised component life cycle), as the complete system has been designed or re-configured. In the run-time phase, the system is executed in SOFAnode.

Palladio

The Palladio Component Model (PCM) [Becker *et al.* (2009); Reussner *et al.* (2011)] is more than just an ADL. In its entirety it is a meta-model specifically

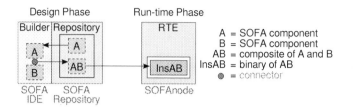

Fig. 6.31   SOFA: component life cycle.

designed to enable quality of service (QoS) prediction, especially performance and reliability, for component-based architectures described by its ADL.

In the ADL part, PCM defines components and composition like UML 2.x (Fig. 6.32). Components are architectural units with provided and required interfaces, and are composed by assembly and delegation connectors.

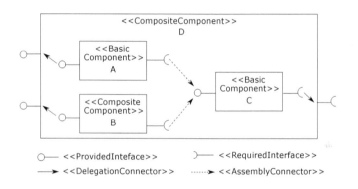

Fig. 6.32   Palladio: components and composition.

Components are specified at different levels of concreteness in terms of implementation, leading to three component types: *provided type* (with only provided interface), *complete type* (with both provided and required interfaces), and *implementation type*, in ascending order of concreteness of specification. The behaviour of a component is specified by a Service Effect Specification (Fig. 6.33), which is basically a state chart or an activity diagram.

As a meta-model, PCM involves many more roles than component and system developers, and many more models than models for components and systems, as well as associated activities. Figure 6.34 shows the roles, models and activities surrounding a PCM architecture (PCM instance in the picture).

Component developers deposit their components' specifications and implementations into a repository, which are accessed by other component developers

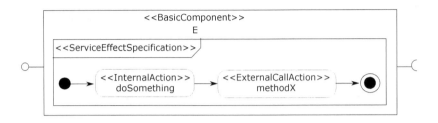

Fig. 6.33   Palladio: component behaviour specification.

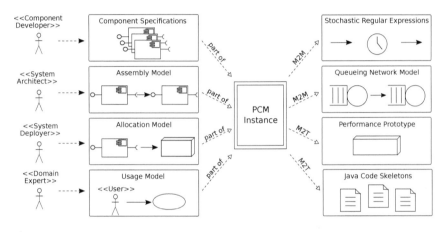

Fig. 6.34   Palladio: roles, models and activities [Becker *et al.* (2009)].

to create composite components, or by software architects to compose systems. System deployers model a system's environment, whereas domain experts supply a description of the users' behaviour, which is necessary for QoS predictions. Specifications from component developers, system architects, system deployers and domain experts are transformed into analytical, simulation-based models for quality analysis.

For the purpose of QoS analyses, component specifications must contain information about system resource usage, *i.e.* the number of CPU cycles demanded by a specific operation within a service or the number of bytes read from or written to an I/O device. Since components are developed without a specific deployment context, such specifications are made against abstract resource types. Only software architects and system deployers know the concrete resources the component will be used on and can define a specific deployment context.

For *performance analysis*, PCM supports model transformation into a discrete-event simulation (SimuCom [Becker *et al.* (2009)]) or layered queuing networks [Koziolek and Reussner (2008)] to derive response times, throughputs, and resource utilisations. For *reliability analysis*, PCM enables a model transformation into absorbing discrete Markov chains [Meyn and Tweedie (2012)] to calculate the *mean time to failure* (the expected time to failure for a non-repairable system) and *mean time to repair* (the total time required for a device to fail and that failure to be repaired), and a reliability simulation to derive the *probability of failure on demand* (the likelihood that the system will fail when a service request is made) for a usage scenario. Finally, for *cost analysis* PCM calculates and adds the cost for each component and resource based on the PCM architecture's annotations to derive the overall expected initial and operational cost for the architecture.

For performance prediction in general, designer friendly performance modelling notations, e.g. UML profile for Schedulability, Performance, and Time [OMG (2005)], and UML profile for Modelling and Analysis of Real-time Embedded Systems [OMG (2011)] are available. Specifically for component-based performance prediction, several approaches are also available (see [Isa *et al.* (2013)] for details and comparisons).

In terms of the idealised component life cycle, in the design phase, (basic and composite) Palladio components are abstractly or concretely defined, built and assembled in the PCM tool, and then stored in the repository of the PCM tool (Fig. 6.35). Complete systems are also assembled in the design phase. For a

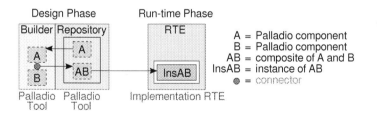

Fig. 6.35   Palladio: component life cycle.

system, a system code skeleton is generated and then implemented using implementation languages such as Java. There is no more composition after the design phase, and therefore there is no deployment phase (PCM system deployers deploy components in the design phase of the idealised component life cycle). In the run-time phase, the complete system implementation is executed in the run-time environment of the chosen implementation language.

Acme

Historically, due to a proliferation of (first-generation) ADLs (*e.g.* Adage [Coglianese and Szymanski (1993)], MetaH [Binns and Vestal (1993)], Aesop [Garlan *et al.* (1994)], Rapide [Luckham *et al.* (1995)], Darwin [Magee *et al.* (1995)], UniCon [Shaw *et al.* (1995)], C2 [Medvidovic *et al.* (1996)] and Wright [Allen and Garland (1997)]) and their supporting tool-sets, there was the need to identify their common foundation of concepts and concerns in a base ADL that served as an interchange language. Acme was designed for this purpose. In its entirety, Acme is built on a core ontology of seven types of entities for architectural representation, namely: *components, connectors, systems, ports, roles, representation and rep-maps*.

To support hierarchical definition of components and connectors, Acme endows their description by one or more detailed *representation*. The use of multiple representations allows Acme to encode multiple views of architectural entities. However, there is nothing built into Acme that supports the resolution of interview correspondences.

A *rep-map*, or representation-map, details the relationships between a system's internal representation and the external interfaces of the component or connector being represented. In the simplest case a *rep-map* details an association between internal and external ports of a component, or internal and external roles for a connector.

To document semantic information about a system relevant to its design and analysis, Acme supports the annotation of architectural elements with arbitrary lists of *properties*. For instance, a property can document the protocol of interaction used by a connector. Since different ADLs focus on different properties (*e.g.* latency, throughput), Acme treats properties as an uninterpreted type, as they become useful when tools use them for analysis, translation, display and manipulation.

Moreover, in order to determine how a system can evolve over time, Acme supports design constraints expressed as predicates over architectural elements. In general a *constraint* represents a claim about an architectural design that should remain true as it evolves over time. For instance, the constraint *Connected(comp1,comp2)* validates that *comp1* is connected to *comp2* by at least one connector.

UML

UML is defined by the Object Management Group (OMG), an international, open membership, not-for-profit technology standards consortium. See http://www.omg.org/. At the time of writing, the current version of UML's specifications is the 2.5. See http://www.omg.org/spec/UML/2.5/PDF.

In UML 1.1 a component is a physical artefact of implementation, e.g. a library, a package, a file, etc.

In UML 1.5 a component is defined as a modular, deployable, and replaceable part of a system that encapsulates implementation and exposes a set of interfaces.

In UML 2.0 a component is defined as a modular unit of the system, with well-defined interfaces, that is replaceable within its environment.

Structured classifiers introduced in UML 2.0 are Class, Collaboration and Component. From being physical artefacts in UML 1.1, components in UML 2.x have become logical entities that are structured classes. A comparison between UML 1.x components and UML 2.0 components can be found in [Bruel and Ober (2006)].

Chapter 7

Component Models with Encapsulated Components

In object-oriented programming, a key desideratum when designing classes is encapsulation. This means controlling data access and hiding information (in particular implementation). The motivation for encapsulation is to design good code that is well-structured, readable, extensible and maintainable. In the context of component-based software development, composition of components being a key concern means that controlling data access and information hiding are not the only aspects of encapsulation that are desirable. An even more crucial aspect of encapsulation is its compositionality, i.e. its preservation through composition. In other words, encapsulation needs to be defined at component level in such a way that the same definition holds at the level of a composite that results from composition. This means that encapsulation needs to have the right semantics, over and above code design guidelines for data access and information hiding.

In this chapter, we describe a component model, called X-MAN, with encapsulated components where encapsulation means 'enclosing behaviour in a capsule', and composition produces composites that preserve this property. These encapsulated components have no external dependencies, and do not invoke one another. They have only provided services and no required services. As a result, they need to be composed exogenously by coordinators. A complete system is a set of encapsulated components composed by a set of coordinators, the system's behaviour being initiated by the top-level coordinator.

As in Chapter 5 and Chapter 6, we will also analyse the component life cycle in X-MAN, and compare it to the idealised component life cycle (Section 1.1), in order to see how well the component model supports the latter.

7.1   X-MAN

X-MAN [Lau *et al.* (2005, 2006); Velasco Elizondo and Lau (2010); He *et al.* (2012); Lau and Tran (2012); di Cola *et al.* (2015)] is a component model with encapsulated components. An X-MAN component has only provided services and no required ones. It provides a set of services through its interface (Fig. 7.1). These services are implemented by methods defined within the component, and

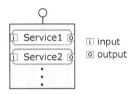

Fig. 7.1   An X-MAN component provides services.

can be invoked only by (exogenous) composition connectors (see below) but not by other components.

X-MAN components can be (i) atomic or (ii) composite (Fig. 7.2). An atomic component (Fig. 7.2(a)) contains a computation unit and an invocation connector. The computation unit performs computation. It provides methods that implement

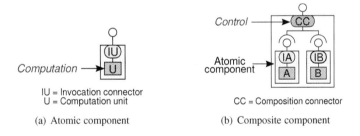

Fig. 7.2   X-MAN: components.

the provided services of the component. The invocation connector invokes these methods in order to yield the provided services. An atomic component is encapsulated in the sense that all its computation occurs within its computation unit, i.e. an atomic component does not invoke the methods of other components. Encapsulation thus means 'enclosure in a capsule'.

Figure 7.3 depicts a Bank atomic component, which provides three services, namely *withdraw*, *balance* and *deposit*. Each service has input and output data, depicted as input and output parameters respectively. For instance, the *withdraw*

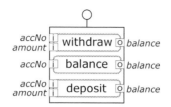

Fig. 7.3   A bank atomic component in X-MAN.

service, takes as input an account number (*accNo*) and the amount to be withdrawn (*withdraw*). It provides the updated *balance* as output.

A composite component (Fig. 7.2(b)) is built from atomic components by composition connectors (Fig. 7.4). A composition connector coordinates control (as well as data flow) between components, i.e. it coordinates the invocation of services between components. Like an atomic component, a composite component is also encapsulated, and it also has only provided services; this is a direct consequence of the encapsulation of an atomic component. Thus in X-MAN encapsulation is preserved by composition. Composite components are self-similar, and indeed composition is algebraic and hierarchical.

A composition connector is a control structure (Fig. 7.4). There are two composition connectors: (i) *sequencer*, which provides sequencing; (ii) *selector*, which provides branching.

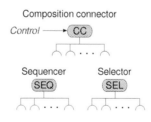

Fig. 7.4   X-MAN: composition connectors.

There are other connectors in X-MAN. There is an *aggregator* connector that aggregates components into a composite with a façade interface. There are also adaptors, e.g. *guard* and *loop*, that are applied to single components. Indeed, the set of all X-MAN connectors is Turing-complete since it includes the control structures for sequencing, branching and looping.

An example of an X-MAN system is shown in Fig. 7.5.[1] It realises a simplified ATM system, which consists of three atomic components (*Reader, Bank A*

---

[1] Data flow between parameters has been omitted for clarity.

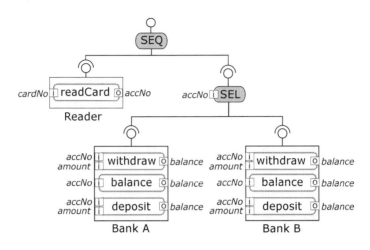

Fig. 7.5   A simplified ATM system in X-MAN.

and Bank B) composed by two connectors (*SEQ, SEL*). When a request arrives, SEQ firstly invokes the service *readCard* to obtain the account number. Secondly, it delegates control to the selector *SEL*, which according to the provided *accNo* invokes the required services from either *Bank A* or *Bank B*.

In terms of the idealised component life cycle, X-MAN supports composition in both the design phase and the deployment phase. In the design phase, in the X-MAN tool [di Cola *et al.* (2015)], components (both atomic and composite) are built in the builder of the tool and deposited in the repository of the tool. This is illustrated in Fig. 7.6. In the deployment phase, components (both atomic and

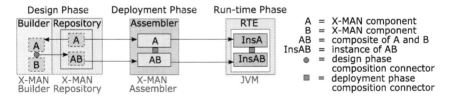

Fig. 7.6   X-MAN: component life cycle.

composite) are retrieved from the repository and composed into a system in the assembler. Since in the tool components are implemented in Java, the resulting system is executed in the Java virtual machine in the run-time phase.

Discussion and Further Reading

Composition connectors in X-MAN are an example of exogenous composition that is algebraic (Fig. 3.14 in Section 3.3). They can also be defined as mathematical operators (Fig. 3.16 in Section 3.4)). This means that in X-MAN, system construction can be performed by hierarchical composition. Hierarchical composition can potentially tackle scale and complexity not only in system construction but also in V&V [He *et al.* (2012)]. Compositional V&V will be crucial for very large systems that require safety. A topical example is obviously the Internet of Things. Other examples are avionic and automotive systems, including driverless cars.

Web Services

In contrast to X-MAN components, web services are not encapsulated components. However, they are composed by coordination (Section 3.2.4), like X-MAN components. For this reason, we describe them here, even though, unlike exogenous composition in X-MAN, coordination of web services is not algebraic (Fig. 3.14 in Section 3.3), and cannot be defined as mathematical operators (Fig. 3.16 in Section 3.4).

Web services [Newcomer (2002); Alonso *et al.* (2004); Barry (2013)] are *web application components* designed to support interoperable machine-to-machine interactions for resource sharing over a network through Internet-based protocols [Sheng *et al.* (2014)]. As such, they are fundamental elements of distributed applications in Service-Oriented Computing [Erl (2005)].

A web service is deployed on a web server and implements functionalities or operations that can be invoked remotely via its interface. As illustrated in Fig. 7.7, a web service contains:

- an *interface* defined by an API description language such as WSDL (Web Service Description Language), WADL (Web Application Description Language) or OpenAPI Specification) [Christensen *et al.* (2001); Chinnici *et al.* (2016b,a)] that describes the functionalities it provides by exposing an arbitrary set of operations;
- a *binary implementation* (the *service code*) of its functionalities.

There are two main kinds of web services: the traditional SOAP-based web services [Scribner *et al.* (2000)] and the conceptually simpler RESTful web

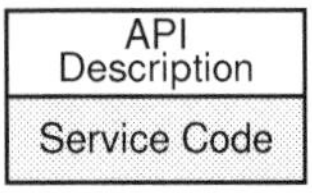

Fig. 7.7   A web service.

services [Dustdar and Schreiner (2005)]. SOAP stands for Simple Object Access Protocol,[2] while REST stands for Representational State Transfer.

SOAP-based web services are typically used to integrate complex enterprise applications. Such a service is defined by WSDL (Web Service Description Language) [Chinnici *et al.* (2016b,a)]. Service registration, discovery and invocation are implemented by SOAP calls, via UDDI (Universal Description, Discovery, and Integration) [Bellwood *et al.* (2002)]. SOAP-based web services are protocol independent and stateful, but demand more computation resources, especially when handling SOAP messages.

RESTful web services were introduced as an architectural style for building large-scale distributed hypermedia systems [Fielding (2000)]. They are identified by URIs, which offer a global addressing space for resource and service discovery. RESTful Web services interact through a uniform interface, which comprises a fixed set of operations in the context of the Web and the Hypertext Transfer Protocol (HTTP): GET, PUT, DELETE and POST. Services interact by exchanging request and response messages, each of which includes enough information to describe how to process the message. In contrast to SOAP-based Web services, RESTful Web services are lightweight and stateless, which are well suited for tactical, ad hoc integration over the Web. A popular technique is mashup that enables users to create situational applications based on existing application components [Ngu *et al.* (2010)].

In summary, a SOAP-based web service has an interface in WSDL that exposes an arbitrary set of operations; whereas a RESTful web service has an interface in WADL (Web Application Description Language) and/or WSDL that describes the functionalities it provides using a uniform set of operations in terms of HTTP verbs, *i.e.* GET, PUT, DELETE and POST. Figure 7.8 compares the functionalities provided by a *Bank* web service in both SOAP and RESTful.

Web services are composed by method calls through SOAP or JSON (JavaScript Object Notation [Bray (2014)]) messages. The interaction among different services can either be centrally orchestrated by a single end point (Fig. 7.9), or distributed among participants of a service choreography (Fig. 7.10).

---

[2]https://www.w3.org/TR/soap/

Service	SOAP web service	RESTful web service
Withdraw money	withdraw(String accNo, Float amount)	www.myBank.uk/account/{id} [PUT]
Show balance	balance(String accNo)	www.myBank.uk/account/{id} [GET]
Deposit money	deposit(String accNo, Float amount)	www.myBank.uk/account/{id} [PUT]

Fig. 7.8   An example of SOAP and RESTful based provided services.

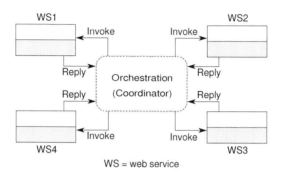

Fig. 7.9   Web service composition: orchestration.

Specifically, web service orchestration is the composition of web services following a defined workflow that is executed on a centralised workflow engine (see Section 3.2.4 and Fig. 3.12 for details and example). In contrast, web service choreography is not executed but enacted when its participants execute their roles [Foster *et al.* (2006)].

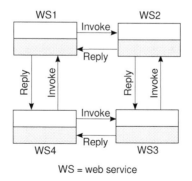

Fig. 7.10   Web service composition: choreography.

Web service choreography is a less well explored approach to web service composition. Indeed, the majority of workflow systems tackle the composition of web services through orchestration, with Business Process Execution Language (WS-BPEL) being the *de facto* standard notation [Jordan *et al.* (2007)].

In terms of the idealised component life cycle, in the design phase, web services are built in a programming environment, e.g. JOpera for Eclipse [Pautasso (2009)], packaged and subsequently deposited on a web server, e.g. Tomcat; the latter being the repository. There is no composition in design phase (Fig. 7.11).

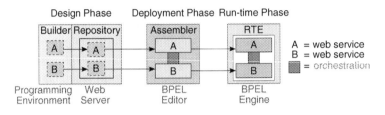

Fig. 7.11   Web services (orchestration): component life cycle.

In the deployment phase, web services are retrieved from servers and composed by orchestration or choreography. In choreography, web services are not assembled. In orchestration, they are composed by a workflow defined in a BPEL editor. At run-time, the resulting workflow is executed on a BPEL engine. Figure 7.11 shows deployment and run-time phases for web service orchestration.

Acknowledgement

We wish to thank Cesare Pautasso for helpful information and discussions.

Chapter 8

A Taxonomy of Software Component Models

In the previous chapters we have presented three categories of component models. These categories are based on the kinds of components defined by the models, namely objects, architectural units and encapsulated components. This categorisation provides a taxonomy of the component models, but a more meaningful and significant taxonomy would be one based on the idealised component life cycle (Section 1.1), since the latter embodies the desiderata of CBD. In this chapter we present such a taxonomy. In the previous chapters we have analysed every model from the point of view of the idealised component life cycle. In this chapter we will use this analysis in the taxonomy.

In general terms, to fully realise the benefits of CBD, we need to have methodologies with components and composition mechanisms, i.e. component models, that fully support the idealised component life cycle. The key desideratum that this life cycle targets is that composition should be possible in both design phase and deployment phase. Realising this desideratum means maximising reuse since composition engenders reuse. Furthermore, as we saw in Section 1.4, the idealised component life cycle supports the W model that defines a component life cycle as well as a system life cycle that together comprise a process for compositional V& V. Compositional V& V is an important desideratum for large complex systems as it can tackle scale and complexity.

Now we classify the component models presented in the previous chapters into a taxonomy with five categories. The taxonomy is shown in Fig. 8.1.

In Fig. 8.1, the first four columns of characteristics are design phase characteristics, while the last one refers to deployment phase characteristics. In the design phase, 'Deposit-N' stands for 'new components can be deposited in a repository'; 'Retrieve' stands for 'components can be retrieved from the repository; 'Compose' stands for 'composition is possible; and 'Deposit-C' stands for 'composite

Category	Component Models	Design			Deploy	
		Deposit-N	Retrieve	Compose	Deposit-C	Compose
Design without Repository	POJOs, Acme ArchJava, UML2.0	✗	✗	✓	✗	✗
Design with Deposit-only Repository	EJB, OSGi, .NET COM, CCM, FRACTAL	✓	✗	✓	✗	✗
Deployment with Repository	JavaBeans Web Services	✓	✗	✗	✗	✓
Design with Repository	KobrA, ProCom, Koala SCA, SOFA, Palladio	✓	✓	✓	✓	✗
Design & Deployment with Repository	X-MAN	✓	✓	✓	✓	✓

Fig. 8.1   Categories based on idealised component life cycle.

components can be deposited in the repository'. In the deployment phase, 'Compose' stands for 'composition is possible'.

8.1   Category 1: Design without Repository

In Category 1 (Fig. 8.2), in the design phase, there is no repository. Therefore components are all constructed from scratch. Composition is possible, and indeed

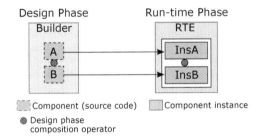

Fig. 8.2   Category 1: design without repository (POJOs, Acme, ArchJava, UML 2.0).

the whole system is (designed and) constructed by composing all the components. There is no deployment phase, i.e. no new composition is possible after the design phase, and the composition of the component instances in the run-time phase is the same as that of the components in the design phase. POJOs and all simple Acme-like ADLs, e.g. ArchJava, belong to this category, as does UML2.0 which is also based on Acme. This category can be described as Design without Repository.

It is easy to see that the component life cycle in POJOs (Fig. 8.3, which is a copy of Fig. 5.1) is indeed an instance of the component life cycle in Category 1 (Fig. 8.2), with method call as the design phase composition operator.

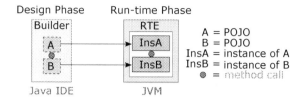

Fig. 8.3   POJOs: component life cycle.

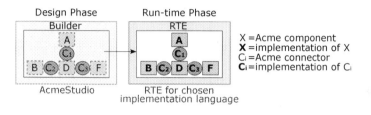

Fig. 8.4   Acme: component life cycle.

Similarly, the component life cycle in Acme (Fig. 8.4, which is a copy of Fig. 6.5) can also be seen to be an instance of the component life cycle in Category 1 (Fig. 8.2), with connector definition as the design phase composition operator and connector implementation as the run-time phase composition operator.

The component life cycle in ArchJava (Fig. 8.5, which is a copy of Fig. 6.10) is the same as that in Acme, except that components and connectors (which are both Java classes/objects) are composed by method calls, in both the design phase

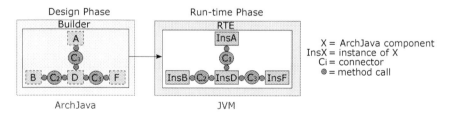

Fig. 8.5   ArchJava: component life cycle.

and the run-rime phase. So it is also an instance of the component life cycle in Category 1 (Fig. 8.2).

In UML 2.x, the component life cycle (Fig. 8.6, which is a copy of Fig. 6.15) is the same as that in ArchJava, except that in the design phase components and connectors are just designs (UML diagrams) and are therefore not composed by any

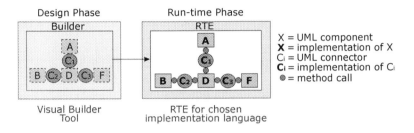

Fig. 8.6   UML 2.x: component life cycle.

code. In the run-time phase, however, components and connectors are composed by some object-oriented code for method calls, like in ArchJava. So the component life cycle in UML 2.x is also an instance of the component life cycle in Category 1 (Fig. 8.2).

8.2   Category 2: Design with Deposit-only Repository

In Category 2 (Fig. 8.7), in the design phase, new components can be (built in a builder and) deposited in a repository, but cannot be retrieved from it.

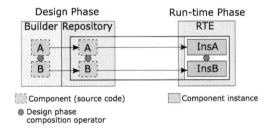

Fig. 8.7   Category 2:   design with deposit-only repository (EJB, OSGi, .NET, COM, CCM, FRACTAL).

Composition is possible, i.e. composites can be formed, but composites cannot be retrieved from the repository, because they do not have identities of their own. No new composition is possible after the design phase, so there is no deployment phase, and the composition of the component instances in the run-time phase is the same as that of the components in the design phase. This category includes EJB, OSGi, .Net, COM, CCM and FRACTAL. It can be described as Design with Deposit-only Repository.

It is easy to see that the component life cycle in EJB (Fig. 8.8, which is a copy of Fig. 5.8) is an instance of the component life cycle in Category 2 (Fig. 8.7). In the design phase, components (EJBs) are designed, implemented, composed (by method calls) and deposited in an EJB container, which serves as a repository.

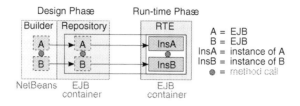

Fig. 8.8   Enterprise JavaBeans: component life cycle.

Components cannot be retrieved from the container, and no more composition is possible. In the run-time phase, component instances are executed in the container, with the same composition defined for the components in the design phase. The component life cycle in OSGi (Fig. 8.9, which is a copy of Fig. 5.12) is the same as that in EJB, except that components are POJOs in bundles. In the

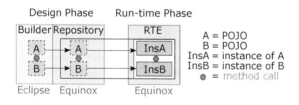

Fig. 8.9   OSGi: component life cycle.

design phase, POJOs in OSGi bundles are constructed in any editor, e.g. Eclipse. They are composed (by method calls) inside a bundle to provide a service (exposed by the bundle). Bundles, and hence POJOs therein, are installed in an OSGi-compliant framework, e.g. Equinox, which is therefore the repository for POJOs. There is no further composition and therefore POJO instances have the same composition as POJOs in the design phase, when they are executed in the run-time phase in the chosen framework.

The component life cycle in .NET (Fig. 8.10, which is a copy of Fig. 5.17) is also the same. In the design phase, .NET components (classes) are constructed

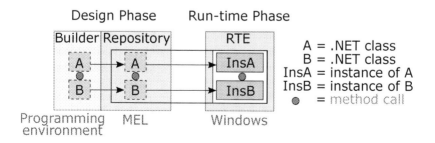

Fig. 8.10   .NET: component life cycle.

and composed (by method calls) in a programming environment such as Microsoft Visual Studio .NET, and stored in the Microsoft Enterprise Library (MEL) on a Windows server. No further composition takes place, and therefore instances of .NET classes have the same composition as .NET classes in the design phase, when they are executed in the run-time phase in Windows.

COM has the same component life cycle (Fig. 8.11, which is a copy of Fig. 5.20). In the design phase, COM components are constructed and composed

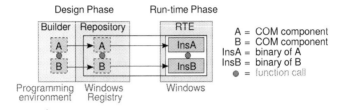

Fig. 8.11   COM: component life cycle.

(by function calls) in a programming environment such as Microsoft Visual Studio, and stored in the Windows Registry on a Windows server. No further composition occurs, and therefore in the run-time phase, binaries of COM components have the same composition as COM components in the design phase, when executed in Windows.

CCM also has the same component life cycle (Fig. 8.12, which is a copy of Fig. 5.24). In the design phase, CCM components are constructed and composed

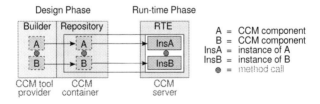

Fig. 8.12   CCM: component life cycle.

(by method calls) in a CCM tool such as OpenCCM, and deposited into a CCM container, hosted and managed by a CCM platform such as OpenCCM. No further composition takes place, and therefore in the run-time phase, instances of CCM components have the same composition as the CCM components in the design phase, when executed on a CCM server.

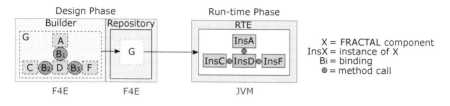

Fig. 8.13   FRACTAL: component life cycle.

In FRACTAL, the component life cycle (Fig. 8.13, which is a copy of Fig. 6.26), in the design phase, FRACTAL components are designed and composed (by interface bindings) into the architecture of the complete system, in the FRACTAL for Eclipse (F4E) IDE, which also serves as a deposit-only repository for the system. No more composition takes place after the design phase, and therefore in the run-time phase, instances of FRACTAL components are composed (by method calls) in the same way as the FRACTAL components are composed (by interface bindings) in the design phase, when executed on a JVM. The component life cycle in FRACTAL is therefore an instance of the component life cycle in Category 2 (Fig. 8.7).

8.3   Category 3: Deployment with Repository

In Category 3 (Fig. 8.14), in the design phase, new components can be (built in a builder and) deposited in a repository, but cannot be retrieved from it. Compo-

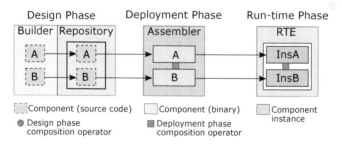

Fig. 8.14   Category 3: deployment with repository (JavaBeans, Web Services).

sition is not possible in the design phase, i.e. no composites can be formed, and so no composites can be deposited in the repository. In the deployment phase, components can be retrieved from the repository, and their binaries formed and composed in an assembler. The composition of the component instances in the run-time phase is that defined for the components (binaries) in the deployment phase. The members of this category JavaBeans and Web Services. This category can be described as Deployment with Repository.

The component life cycle in JavaBeans (Fig. 8.15, which is a copy of Fig. 5.5) is clearly an instance of the component life cycle in Category 3 (Fig. 8.14). In the

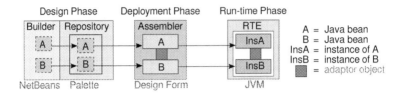

Fig. 8.15   JavaBeans: component life cycle.

design phase, beans are constructed in a visual bean builder tool like NetBeans, and deposited in a repository (as JAR files) such as the Palette in NetBeans, but they cannot be composed at this stage. They are composed in deployment phase in a canvas (which serves as an assembler) such as the Design Form in NetBeans, after being retrieved from the repository. In the run-time phase, the composition of the bean instances is the same as the composition of beans in the deployment phase, when executed on a JVM.

The component life cycle in web services using orchestration for composition (Fig. 8.16, which is a copy of Fig. 7.11) is also an instance of the component life cycle in Category 3. In the design phase, individual web services are designed and

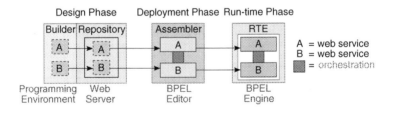

Fig. 8.16   Web services: component life cycle.

implemented in a programming environment, and then packaged and deposited on a web server, which serves as a repository. There is no composition in the design phase. In the deployment phase, web services are identified and retrieved from their host web servers and composed by orchestration on a BPEL editor into a workflow. In the run-time phase, this workflow is executed on the BPEL engine. The composition of the web services is as defined in the deployment phase.

8.4 Category 4: Design with Repository

In Category 4 (Fig. 8.17), in the design phase, new components can be (built in a builder and) deposited in a repository, and components can be retrieved from the repository. Composition is possible, and composites, including complete systems, can be deposited in the repository. No further composition takes place, and there-

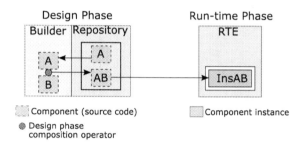

Fig. 8.17 Category 4: design with repository (ProCom, Koala, SCA, SOFA, KobrA, Palladio).

fore there is no deployment phase. In the run-time phase, the composition of the component instances is the same as that of the components in the design phase. ProCom, Koala, SCA, SOFA, KobrA, and Palladio belong to this category. This category can be described as Design with Repository.

It is easy to see that the component life cycle in ProCom (Fig. 8.18, which is a copy of Fig. 6.19) is an instance of the component life cycle in Category 4

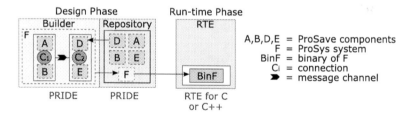

Fig. 8.18 ProCom: component life cycle.

(Fig. 8.17). In the design phase in ProCom, new ProSave components (A, B, D, E in Fig. 8.18) can be built in the PRIDE tool and deposited in the repository of the tool. These ProSave components can be retrieved from the repository and composed (by connectors) into Prosave composites, which in turn can be composed (by message channels) into a ProSys component or a complete system (F in Fig. 8.18). No further composition takes place after the design phase, so there is no deployment phase. In the run-time phase, the ProSys system has the same composition as that defined in the design phase.

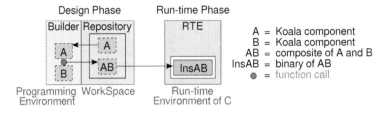

Fig. 8.19   Koala: component life cycle.

The component life cycle in Koala (Fig. 8.19, which is a copy of Fig. 6.23) is clearly an instance of the component life cycle in Category 4 (Fig. 8.17). In the design phase, Koala components (definition files) can be created in a Koala programming environment and deposited in a file system (KoalaModel Workspace). These components can be retrieved from Workspace and composed (by function calls) into composites or complete systems (also definition files). C code for the components has to be written and added to their definition files, but no further composition occurs after the design phase, and therefore there is no deployment phase. In the run-rime phase, the composition of the component instances is as defined for the components in the design phase, when they are executed in the run-time environment of C.

The component life cycle in SCA (Fig. 8.20, which is a copy of Fig. 6.29) is the same as that of Koala. In the design phase, SCA components can be created

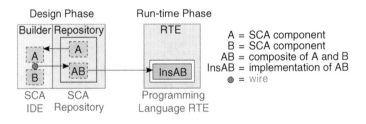

Fig. 8.20   SCA: component life cycle.

in an SCA IDE and deposited in an SCA repository. These components can be retrieved from the repository and composed (by wiring matching services together) into a composite or a complete system. After the design phase, the components (and their composition) have to be implemented, but no further composition takes place, and so there is no deployment phase. In the run-time phase the composition in the implementation is as defined in the design phase, when it is executed in the run-time environment of the chosen implementation language.

The component life cycle in SOFA (Fig. 8.21, which is a copy of Fig. 6.31) is the same as that in Koala and SCA. In the design phase, SOFA components

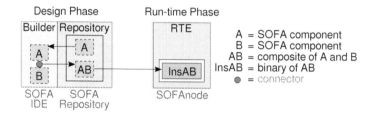

Fig. 8.21   SOFA: component life cycle.

are built in a SOFA IDE, and can be deposited into a SOFA repository. These components can be retrieved from the repository and composed (by connectors that bind their interfaces together) into a composite or a complete system. There is no further composition after the design phase, so there is no deployment phase. In the run-time phase, the composition in the binary of the system is the same as the composition defined in the design phase, when the system is executed in a SOFANode.

The component life cycle in KobrA (Fig. 8.22, which is a copy of Fig. 5.26) is also the same. In the design phase KobrA components are defined (as UML

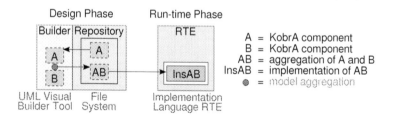

Fig. 8.22   KobrA: component life cycle.

models) in a UML visual builder tool and can be deposited in a file system. These components can be retrieved from the file system and composed (by aggregation) into an aggregate for a system. Object-oriented code has to be written to completely implement the aggregated models, after the design phase, but no more composition (aggregation) occurs, and so there is no deployment phase. In the run-time phase, the composition (by method calls) of objects in the implemented system is the same as that of classes in the aggregation in the design phase, when the implementation is executed in the run-time of the chosen object-oriented language.

The component life cycle in Palladio (Fig. 8.23, which is a copy of Fig. 6.35) is the same again. In the design phase, basic Palladio components are built and

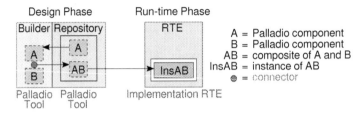

Fig. 8.23   Palladio: component life cycle.

composed (by connectors) in the Palladio, and can be deposited in a repository in the tool. These components can be retrieved from the repository and composed further into composites or a complete system. After the design phase, the implementation of the system has to be completed in a chosen implementation language such as Java, but there is no more composition and therefore there is no deployment phase. In the run-time phase, the composition of the component instances is the same as that of the components in the design phase, when they are executed in the run-time environment of the chosen implementation language.

8.5   Category 5: Design and Deployment with Repository

In Category 5 (Fig. 8.24), in the design phase, new components can be (built in a builder and) deposited in a repository, and components can be retrieved from the repository. Composition is possible, and composites can be built and deposited in the repository. In the deployment phase, composition is also possible, and as a result, the composition of the component instances in the run-time phase can be entirely different from that in the design phase. X-MAN is the sole member of this category. This category can be described as Design and Deployment with Repository.

The component life cycle in X-MAN clearly coincides with that that in Category 5 (Fig. 8.24). In the design phase, new X-MAN components can be built, composed and deposited in the repository. Components in the repository can be retrieved for composition into new composites, which in turn can be deposited in the repository. In the deployment phase, components can be retrieved from the

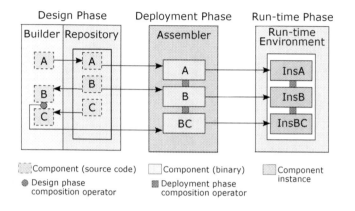

Fig. 8.24 Category 5: design and deployment with repository (X-MAN).

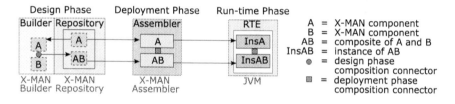

Fig. 8.25 X-MAN: component life cycle.

repository and their binaries can be composed in the assembler. In the run-time phase, the composition of the component instances is the same as that of component binaries in the deployment phase, when executed in the run-time environment (JVM).

Discussion and Further Reading

The basis for the taxonomy in Fig. 8.1 is the idealized component life cycle, as discussed in Section 1.1, which is in turn based on desiderata for CBD [Broy *et al.* (1998); (2001); Szyperski *et al.* (2002); Meyer (2003)]. These desiderata are well established and widely accepted. Indeed, the taxonomy in Fig. 8.1 has been used by other researchers to evaluate and improve their component models, e.g. [Hnětynka and Plášil (2006)].

Looking at the taxonomy, it is interesting to note that among models in the Design with Repository category, Koala and KobrA are intended for product line engineering [Pohl *et al.* (2005); Clements and Northrop (2015)], which has proved to be the most successful approach for software reuse, a key objective and benefit of CBD, in practice. The main reason for its success is precisely its use of repositories of families of components, i.e. product lines.

At the other end of the scale, models in the Design without Repository category are focused on designing (systems and) components from scratch, rather than reusing existing components from a repository.

Models in the categories Design with Deposit-only Repository and Deployment with Repository are different from those in the Design with Repository category in that the former store binary compiled code whereas the latter store units of design in the repository, which are more generic and hence more reusable.

The only component model that has composition in both the design and the deployment phase is X-MAN (Section 7.1). In X-MAN it is possible to retrieve composites for further composition in the deployment phase, which is not possible for models in the Design with Repository category.

Looking forward to the future, there are new desiderata for CBD: foremost among these are *scale*, *complexity* and *safety*. Software is becoming all pervasive, and will only become even more so in future, as the Internet of Things become reality. Safety will be critical as humans are enveloped by software. A striking example is human safety in driverless cars, which are completely controlled by software.

To tackle scale, complexity and safety we need: (i) components that are easy to reuse; (ii) composition mechanisms that will enable systematic composition as well as compositional V&V.

We believe that to achieve these objects, components should have the key properties of *encapsulation* and *compositionality*, like in X-MAN. Encapsulation makes reuse easier because it removes coupling between components. Compositionality enables hierarchical composition, which can tackle scale and complexity.

Objects and architectural units are both lacking in encapsulation and compositionality. Objects encapsulate data, but not control or computation. They are not compositional. Architectural units are compositional and can encapsulate data, but they do not encapsulate control or computation.

By contrast, in X-MAN, encapsulation occurs at every level of composition, and it encapsulates every composite into just an interface. This interface is all we need to know about the composite in order to use it for further composition. This means that we can encapsulate larger and larger composites at each step, and by so doing, we are able to subsequently compose larger and larger composites without any regard for their size or complexity. Consequently, composition is hierarchical in X-MAN and composites are self-similar.

Hierarchical composition in turn enables compositional V&V, following a process like the W model(Section 1.4), which will be able to tackle the V& V of large complex systems.

Finally, as mentioned in Discussion and Further Reading in Chapter 4, a tutorial on component models can be found in [Lau (2014); Lau *et al.* (2014)]. An older tutorial can be found in [Lau (2006a,b)], with further details in [Lau and Wang (2006)].

Acknowledgement

We wish to thank Ivica Crnkovic, David Garlan, Dirk Muthig, Oscar Nierstrasz, Bastiaan Schonhage and Kurt Wallnau for information and helpful discussions.

Bibliography

Achermann, F., Lumpe, M., Schneider, J.-G., and Nierstrasz, O. (2001). Piccola — A small composition language, in H. Bowman and J. Derrick (eds.), *Formal Methods for Distributed Processing — A Survey of Object-Oriented Approaches* (Cambridge University Press), pp. 403–426.

Achermann, F. and Nierstrasz, O. (2005). A calculus for reasoning about software composition, *Theoretical Computer Science* **331**, 2-3, pp. 367–396.

Acme (2011). The Acme architectural description language, http://www.cs.cmu.ed u/~acme/.

AcmeStudio (2009). *AcmeStudio Home Page*, Carnegie Mellon University, http://www .cs.cmu.edu/~acme/AcmeStudio/.

Aldrich, J., Chambers, C., and Notkin, D. (2001). Component-oriented programming in ArchJava, in *First OOPSLA Workshop on Language Mechanisms for Programming Software Components*, pp. 1–8.

Aldrich, J., Chambers, C., and Notkin, D. (2002). ArchJava: Connecting software architecture to implementation, in *Proceedings of International Conference on Software Engineering 2002* (IEEE), pp. 187–197.

Aldrich, J., Garlan, D., Schmerl, B., and Tseng, T. (2004). Modeling and implementing software architecture with Acme and ArchJava, in *Proceedings of OOPSLA Companion 2004*, pp. 156–157.

Allen, R. and Garland, D. (1997). A formal basis for architectural connection, *ACM Transactions on Software Engineering and Methodology* **6**, 3, pp. 213–248.

Alonso, G., Casati, F., Kuno, H., and Machiraju, V. (2004). *Web Services: Concepts, Architectures and Applications* (Springer-Verlag).

Apel, S. and Lengauer, C. (2008). Superimposition: A language-independent approach to software composition, in C. Pautasso and E. Tanter (eds.), *Software Composition, Lecture Notes in Computer Science*, Vol. 4954 (Springer), pp. 20–35.

Arbab, F. (2004). Reo: A channel-based coordination model for component composition, *Mathematical Structures in Computer Science* **14**, 3, pp. 329–366.

Aßmann, U. (2003). *Invasive Software Composition* (Springer).

Atkinson, C., Bayer, J., Bunse, C., Kamsties, E., Laitenberger, O., Laqua, R., Muthig, D., Paech, B., Wüst, J., and Zettel, J. (2001). *Component-Based Product Line Engineering with UML* (Addison-Wesley).

Atkinson, C., Bayer, J., and Muthig, D. (2000). Component-based product line development: The KobrA approach, in *Proceedings of the First Software Product Line Conference* (Springer), pp. 289–309.

Atkinson, C., Bostan, P., Brenner, D., Falcone, G., Gutheil, M., Hummel, O., Juhasz, M., and Stoll, D. (2008). Modeling components and component-based systems in KobrA, in A. Rausch, R. Reussner, R. Mirandola, and F. Plášil (eds.), *The Common Component Modeling Example: Comparing Software Component Models, Lecture Notes in Computer Science*, Vol. 5153 (Springer), pp. 54–84.

Bachmann, F., Bass, L., Buhman, C., Comella-Dorda, S., Long, F., Robert, J., Seacord, R., and Wallnau, K. (2000). Volume II: Technical concepts of component-based software engineering, 2nd edn., Tech. Rep. CMU/SEI-2000-TR-008, CMU/SEI.

Barry, D. K. (2013). *Web Services, Service-Oriented Architectures, and Cloud Computing: The Savvy Manager's Guide*, 2nd edn. (Morgan Kaufmann).

Bartlett, D. (2001). CORBA Component Model (CCM): Introducing next-generation CORBA, http://www-106.ibm.com/developerworks/linux/library/co-cjct6/.

Bass, L., Clements, P., and Kazman, R. (2012). *Software Architecture in Practice*, 3rd edn., SEI Series in Software Engineering (Addison-Wesley).

Batory, D., Singhal, V., Thomas, J., Dasari, S., Geraci, B., and Sirkin, M. (1994). The GenVoca model of software-system generators, *IEEE Software* **11**, 5, pp. 89–94.

BEA Systems *et al.* (1999). CORBA Components, Tech. Rep. orbos/99-02-05, Object Management Group.

Becker, S., Koziolek, H., and Reussner, R. (2009). The Palladio component model for model-driven performance prediction, *Journal of Systems and Software* **82**, 1, pp. 3–22.

Bellwood, T., Capell, S., Clement, L., Colgrave, J., Dovey, M., Feygin, D., Kochman, A., Macias, P., Novotny, M., and Paolucci, M. *et al.* (2002). Universal description, discovery and integration specification (UDDI) 3.0, http://uddi.org/pubs/uddi-v3.00-published-20020719.htm.

Benington, H. D. (1983). Production of large computer programs, *IEEE Annals of the History of Computing* **5**, 4, pp. 350–361.

Binns, P. and Vestal, S. (1993). Formal real-time architecture specification and analysis, *IEEE Real-Time Systems Newsletter* **9**, 1-2, pp. 104–108.

Bolton, F. (2001). *Pure Corba* (Pearson Education).

Box, D. (1998). *Essential COM* (Addison-Wesley).

Bracha, G. and Cook, W. (1990). Mixin-based inheritance, *ACM Sigplan Notices* **25**, 10, pp. 303–311.

Bray, T. (2014). The JavaScript Object Notation (JSON) Data Interchange Format, http://www.rfc-editor.org/info/rfc7159.

Broy, M., Deimel, A., Henn, J., Koskimies, K., Plášil, F., Pomberger, G., Pree, W., Stal, M., and Szyperski, C. (1998). What characterizes a software component? *Software – Concepts and Tools* **19**, 1, pp. 49–56.

Bruel, J.-M. and Ober, I. (2006). Components modelling in UML 2, *Studia Univ. Babeş-Bolyai, Informatica* **LI**, 1, pp. 79–90.

Bruneton, E., Coupaye, T., Leclercq, M., Quéma, V., and Stefani, J.-B. (2006). The FRAC-
TAL component model and its support in Java, *Software: Practice and Experience*
36, 11-12, pp. 1257–1284.

Buchi, M. and Weck, W. (1998). Compound types for Java, in *Proceedings of Conference
on Object-Oriented Programming, Systems, Languages, and Applications* (ACM
Press), pp. 362–373.

Bures, T., Hnetynka, P., and Plášil, F. (2006). SOFA 2.0: Balancing advanced features in a hierarchical component model, in *Proceedings of SERA 2006* (IEEE),
pp. 40–48.

Burke, B. and Monson-Haefel, R. (2006). *Enterprise JavaBeans 3.0*, 5th edn. (O'Reilly &
Associates).

Capretz, L. (2005). Y: A new component-based software life cycle model, *Journal of
Computer Science* **1**, 1, pp. 76–82.

Chaudron, M. (2001). Reflections on the anatomy of software composition languages and
mechanism, in *Proceedings of the Workshop on Composition Languages*.

Cheesman, J. and Daniels, J. (2001). *UML Components: A Simple Process for Specifying
Component-Based Software* (Addison-Wesley).

Chinnici, R., Haas, H., Lewis, A., Moreau, J., Orchard, D., and Weerawarana, S. (2016a).
Web Services Description Language (WSDL) Version 2.0 Part 2: Adjuncts, htt
p://www.w3.org/TR/wsdl20-adjuncts, W3C Recommendation 26 June
2007.

Chinnici, R., Moreau, J., Ryman, A., and Weerawarana, S. (2016b). Web Services Description Language (WSDL) Version 2.0 Part 1: Core Language, http://www.w3.o
rg/TR/wsdl20, W3C Recommendation 26 June 2007.

Choi, Y.-H., Kwon, O.-C., and Shin, G.-S. (2002). An approach to composition of EJB
components using C2 style, in *Proceedings of 28th EUROMICRO Conference*
(IEEE), pp. 40–46.

Christensen, E., Curbera, F., Meredith, G., and Weerawarana, S. (2001). Web Services
Description Language (WSDL) 1.1, Tech. rep., W3C, http://www.bibsonomy
.org/bibtex/27697fadb78aa757322a25fc6252c7a92/neilernst.

Christiansson, B., Jakobsson, L., and Crnkovic, I. (2002). CBD process, in I. Crnkovic and
M. Larsson (eds.), *Building Reliable Component-Based Software Systems* (Artech
House), pp. 89–113.

Clements, P. and Northrop, L. (2015). *Software Product Lines: Practices and Patterns*
(Addison-Wesley).

Clements, P. C. (1996). A survey of architecture description languages, in *Proceedings of
8th International Workshop on Software Specification and Design* (IEEE Computer
Society), pp. 16–25.

Coglianese, L. and Szymanski, R. (1993). DSSA-ADAGE: An environment for
architecture-based avionics development, in *Proceedings of AGARD, Aerospace
Software Engineering for Advanced Systems Architectures*.

Cox, B. (1986). *Object-Oriented Programming: An Evolutionary Approach* (Addison-
Wesley).

Crnkovic, I., Chaudron, M., and Larsson, S. (2006). Component-based development
process and component lifecycle, in *Proceedings of International Conference on
Software Engineering Advances*, pp. 44–53.

Crnkovic, I., Sentilles, S., Vulgarakis, A., and Chaudron, M. (2011). A classification framework for software component models, *IEEE Transactions on Software Engineering* **37**, 5, pp. 593–615, doi:10.1109/TSE.2010.83.

Czarnecki, K. and Eisenecker, U. (2000). *Generative Programming: Methods, Tools, and Applications* (ACM Press/Addison-Wesley Publishing Co.).

da Cruz, M. F. and Raistrick, P. (2007). AMBERS: Improving requirements specification through assertive models and SCADE/DOORS integration, in F. Redmill and T. Anderson (eds.), *The Safety of Systems, Proceedings of 15th Safety-critical Systems Symposium* (Springer London), pp. 217–241.

DeMichiel, L., Yalçinalp, L., and Krishnan, S. (2001). *Enterprise JavaBeans Specification Version 2.0*, Sun Microsystems.

DeRemer, F. and Kron, H. (1976). Programming-in-the-large versus programming-in-the-small, *IEEE Transactions on Software Engineering* **2**, 2, pp. 80–86.

di Cola, S., Tran, C., and Lau, K.-K. (2015). A graphical tool for model-driven development using components and services, in *Proceedings of 41st Euromicro Conference on Software Engineering and Advanced Applications (SEAA) 2015*, pp. 181–182.

Ducasse, S., Nierstrasz, O., Schärli, N., Wuyts, R., and Black, A. (2006). Traits: A mechanism for fine-grained reuse, *ACM Transactions on Programming Languages and Systems* **28**, 2, pp. 331–388.

Dustdar, S. and Schreiner, W. (2005). A survey on web services composition, *International Journal of Web and Grid Services* **1**, 1, pp. 1–30.

EAST-ADL Association (2016). EAST-ADL http://www.east-adl.info/Specification.html.

Englander, R. (1997). *Developing Java Beans* (O'Reilly & Associates).

Erl, T. (2005). *Service-Oriented Architecture: Concepts, Technology, and Design* (Prentice Hall).

Esposito, D. and Saltarello, A. (2014). *Microsoft .NET: Architecting Applications for the Enterprise*, 2nd edn. (Microsoft Press).

Evans, B. and Flanagan, D. (2014). *Java in a Nutshell* (O'Reilly Media, Inc.).

Fielding, R. T. (2000). *Architectural Styles and the Design of Network-based Software Architectures*, Ph.D. thesis, University of California, Irvine.

Flatt, M., Krishnamurthi, S., and Felleisen, M. (1999). A programmer's reduction semantics for classes and mixins, in J. Alves-Foss (ed.), *Formal Syntax and Semantics of Java* (Springer-Verlag), pp. 241–269.

Foster, H., Uchitel, S., Magee, J., and Kramer, J. (2006). Model-based analysis of obligations in web service choreography, in *Proceedings of International Conference on Internet and Web Applications and Services* (IEEE), pp. 149–149.

Fowler, M., Parsons, R., and MacKenzie, J. (2009). POJO: An acronym for: Plain Old Java Object, https://www.martinfowler.com/bliki/POJO.html.

Garlan, D., Allen, R., and Ockerbloom, J. (1994). Exploiting style in architectural design environments, *ACM SIGSOFT Software Engineering Notes* **19**, 5, pp. 175–188.

Garlan, D., Monroe, R., and Wile, D. (2000). Acme: Architectural description of component-based systems, in G. Leavens and M. Sitaraman (eds.), *Foundations of Component-Based Systems* (Cambridge University Press), pp. 47–68.

Garlan, D., Monroe, R., and Wile, D. (2010). Acme: An architecture description interchange language, in *CASCON First Decade High Impact Papers* (IBM Corp.), pp. 159–173.

Gaufillet, A. and Gabel, B. (2010). Avionic software development with TOPCASED SAM, in *Proceedings of Embedded Real Time Software and Systems 2010*.

Gédéon, W. (2010). *OSGi and Apache Felix 3.0* (Packt Publishing Ltd).

Gelernter, D. and Carriero, N. (1992). Coordination languages and their significance, *Communications of ACM* **35**, 2, pp. 97–107.

Goebel, S. and Nestler, M. (2004). Composite component support for EJB, in *Proceedings of the Winter International Symposium on Information and Communication Technologies*, pp. 1–6.

Hall, R., Pauls, K., McCulloch, S., and Savage, D. (2011). *OSGi in Action: Creating Modular Applications in Java* (Manning Publications Co.).

Harrison, W. H., Ossher, H., and Tarr, P. (2002). Asymmetrically vs. symmetrically organized paradigms for software composition, Research Report RC22685, IBM Thomas J. Watson Research.

He, N., Kroening, D., Wahl, T., Lau, K.-K., Taweel, F., Tran, C., Rümmer, P., and Sharma, S. (2012). Component-based design and verification in X-MAN, in *Proceedings of Embedded Real Time Software and Systems*.

Heffelfinger, D. R. (2014). *Java EE 7 with GlassFish 4 Application Server* (Packt Publishing Ltd).

Heineman, G. T. and Councill, W. T. (eds.) (2001). *Component-Based Software Engineering: Putting the Pieces Together* (Addison-Wesley).

Hnětynka, P. and Plášil, F. (2006). Dynamic reconfiguration and access to services in hierarchical component models, in I. Gorton, G. T. Heineman, I. Crnkovic, H. W. Schmidt, J. A. Stafford, C. A. Szyperski, and K. C. Wallnau (eds.), *Proceedings of 9th International Symposium on Component-Based Software Engineering, Lecture Notes in Computer Science*, Vol. 4063 (Springer-Verlag), pp. 352–359.

Hoare, T. (2005). Process algebra: A unifying approach, in *Proceedings of the 2004 International Conference on Communicating Sequential Processes: The First 25 Years*, CSP'04 (Springer-Verlag), pp. 36–60.

IABG (2017). The V-modell. Development standard for IT-systems of the Federal Republic of Germany, IABG, http://www.v-modell.iabg.de.

Isa, M., Zaki, M. Z., and Jawawi, D. N. (2013). A survey of design model for quality analysis: From a performance and reliability perspective, *Computer and Information Science* **6**, 2, p. 55.

Jamae, J. and Johnson, P. (2009). *JBoss in Action: Configuring the JBoss Application Server* (Manning Publications Co.).

JavaBeans Specification (1997). Javabeans Specification, http://java.sun.com/products/javabeans/docs/spec.html.

Jordan, D., Evdemon, J., Alves, A., Arkin, A., Askary, S., Barreto, C., Bloch, B., Curbera, F., Ford, M., and Goland, Y., *et al.* (2007). Web services business process execution language version 2.0, *OASIS Standard* **11**, 120, p. 5.

Kaur, K. and Singh, H. (2010). Candidate process models for component based software development, *Journal of Software Engineering* **4**, 1, pp. 16–29.

Kiczales, G., Hilsdale, E., Hugunin, J., Kersten, M., Palm, J., and Griswold, W. (2001). An overview of AspectJ, in *Proceedings of ECOOP '01* (Springer-Verlag), pp. 327–353.

Kiczales, G., Lamping, J., Mendhekar, A., Maeda, C., Lopes, C., Loingtier, J.-M., and Irwin, J. (1997). Aspect-oriented programming, in *Proceedings of ECOOP'97* (Springer), pp. 220–242.

Kojarski, S. and Lorenz, D. (2006). Modeling aspect mechanisms: A top-down approach, in *Proceedings of 28th International Conference on Software Engineering* (ACM), pp. 212–221.

Kotonya, G., Sommerville, I., and Hall, S. (2003). Towards a classification model for component-based software engineering research, in *Proceedings of 29th EUROMI-CRO Conference 2003, New Waves in System Architecture* (IEEE Computer Society), pp. 43–52.

Koziolek, H. and Reussner, R. (2008). A model transformation from the Palladio component model to layered queueing networks, in *Proceedings of SPEC International Performance Evaluation Workshop* (Springer), pp. 58–78.

Lau, K.-K. (2006a). Software component models, in *Proceedings of 28th International Conference on Software Engineering* (ACM Press), pp. 1081–1082, Abstract of tutorial.

Lau, K.-K. (2006b). Software component models, http://www.cs.man.ac.uk/~k ung-kiu/pub/icse06tut.pdf, Tutorial at 28th International Conference on Software Engineering, 2006, Shanghai, China.

Lau, K.-K. (2014). Software component models: Past, present and future, in *Proceedings of the 17th International ACM SIGSOFT Symposium on Component-Based Software Engineering* (ACM), pp. 185–186, Abstract of tutorial.

Lau, K.-K. and Ornaghi, M. (2009). Control encapsulation: A calculus for exogenous composition, in G. Lewis, I. Poernomo, and C. Hofmeister (eds.), *Proceedings of 12th International Symposium on Component-Based Software Engineering, Lecture Notes in Computer Science*, Vol. 5582 (Springer-Verlag), pp. 121–139.

Lau, K.-K., Ornaghi, M., and Wang, Z. (2006). A software component model and its preliminary formalisation, in F. de Boer *et al.* (ed.), *Proceedings of 4th International Symposium on Formal Methods for Components and Objects, Lecture Notes in Computer Science*, Vol. 4111 (Springer-Verlag), pp. 1–21.

Lau, K.-K. and Rana, T. (2010). A taxonomy of software composition mechanisms, in *Proceedings of 36th EUROMICRO Conference on Software Engineering and Advanced Applications* (IEEE), pp. 102–110.

Lau, K.-K. and Taweel, F. (2009). Domain-specific software component models, in G. Lewis, I. Poernomo, and C. Hofmeister (eds.), *Proceedings of 12th International Symposium on Component-Based Software Engineering, Lecture Notes in Computer Science*, Vol. 5582 (Springer-Verlag), pp. 19–35.

Lau, K.-K. and Tran, C. (2012). X-MAN: An MDE tool for component-based system development, in *Proceedings of 38th EUROMICRO Conference on Software Engineering and Advanced Applications* (IEEE), pp. 158–165.

Lau, K.-K. and Ukis, V. (2006). Defining and checking deployment contracts for software components, in I. Gorton, G. T. Heineman, I. Crnkovic, H. W. Schmidt, J. A. Stafford, C. A. Szyperski, and K. C. Wallnau (eds.), *Proceedings of the*

9th International Symposium on Component-Based Software Engineering, Lecture Notes in Computer Science, Vol. 4063 (Springer), pp. 1–16.

Lau, K.-K., Velasco Elizondo, P., and Wang, Z. (2005). Exogenous connectors for software components, in G. T. Heineman, I. Crnkovic, H. W. Schmidt, J. A. Stafford, C. A. Szyperski, and K. C. Wallnau (eds.), *Proceedings of 8th International Symposium on Component-based Software Engineering, Lecture Notes in Computer Science*, Vol. 3489 (Springer-Verlag), pp. 90–106.

Lau, K.-K. and Wang, Z. (2005). A taxonomy of software component models, in *Proceedings of the 31st Euromicro Conference on Software Engineering and Advanced Applications* (IEEE Computer Society Press), pp. 88–95.

Lau, K.-K. and Wang, Z. (2006). A survey of software component models, http://www .cs.man.ac.uk/~kung-kiu/pub/cspp30.pdf, second edition, Pre-print CSPP-38, School of Computer Science, The University of Manchester, May 2006.

Lau, K.-K. and Wang, Z. (2007). Software component models, *IEEE Transactions on Software Engineering* 33, 10, pp. 709–724.

Lau, K.-K., Wang, Z., di Cola, S., Tran, C., and Christou, V. (2014). Software component models: Past, present and future, http://www.cs.man.ac.uk/~kung-kiu /pub/cbse14tut-slides.pdf, Tutorial at COMPARCH 2014 Conference, 30 June 2014, Lille, France.

Lee, R. and Seligman, S. (2000). *The JNDI API Tutorial and Reference: Building Directory-Enabled Java Applications* (Addison-Wesley Longman Publishing Co., Inc.).

Li, J.-H., Li, Q., and Li, J. (2008). The W-Model for testing software product lines, in *Proceedings of International Symposium on Computer Science and Computational Technology*, pp. 690–693.

Lorenz, D. H. and Petkovic, P. (2000). Design-time assembly of runtime containment components, in *Proceedings of 34th International Conference on Technology of Object-Oriented Languages and Systems* (IEEE), pp. 195–204.

Luckham, D. C., Kenney, J. J., Augustin, L. M., Vera, J., Bryan, D., and Mann, W. (1995). Specification and analysis of system architecture using rapide, *IEEE Transactions on Software Engineering* 21, 4, pp. 336–354.

Lumpe, M., Achermann, F., and Nierstrasz, O. (2000). A formal language for composition, in G. T. Leavens and M. Sitaraman (eds.), *Foundations of Component-Based Systems* (Cambridge University Press), pp. 69–90.

Magee, J., Dulay, N., Eisenbach, S., and Kramer, J. (1995). Specifying distributed software architectures, in *Proceedings of European Software Engineering Conference* (Springer), pp. 137–153.

Maras, J., Lednicki, L., and Crnkovic, I. (2012). 15 years of CBSE Symposium — impact on the research community, in *Proceedings of the 15th International ACM SIGSOFT Symposium on Component-Based Software Engineering* (ACM), pp. 61–70.

Marvie, R. and Merle, P. (2001). CORBA Component Model: Discussion and Use with OpenCCM, Tech. rep., Laboratoire d'Informatique Fondamentale de Lille.

McAffer, J., VanderLei, P., and Archer, S. (2010). *OSGi and Equinox: Creating Highly Modular Java Systems* (Addison-Wesley Professional).

McIlroy, D. (1968). Mass produced software components, in P. Naur and B. Randell (eds.), *Software Engineering*, pp. 138–155.

Medvidovic, N., Dashofy, E. M., and Taylor, R. N. (2007). Moving architectural description from under the technology lamppost, *Information and Software Technology* **49**, 1, pp. 12–31.

Medvidovic, N., Oreizy, P., Robbins, J. E., and Taylor, R. N. (1996). Using object-oriented typing to support architectural design in the c2 style, *ACM SIGSOFT Software Engineering Notes* **21**, 6, pp. 24–32.

Medvidovic, N. and Taylor, R. N. (2000). A classification and comparison framework for software architecture description languages, *IEEE Transactions on Software Engineering* **26**, 1, pp. 70–93.

Mehta, N. R., Medvidovic, N., and Phadke, S. (2000). Towards a taxonomy of software connectors, in *Proceedings of International Conference on Software Engineering*, pp. 178–187.

Meyer, B. (2003). The grand challenge of trusted components, in *Proceedings of International Conference on Software Engineering* (IEEE Computer Society), pp. 660–667.

Meyn, S. P. and Tweedie, R. L. (2012). *Markov Chains and Stochastic Stability* (Springer Science & Business Media).

Mishra, P. and Dutt, N. (2011). Introduction to architecture description languages, in *Processor Description Languages: Applications and Methodologies* (Morgan Kaufmann), pp. 1–12.

Natan, R. (1995). *CORBA: A Guide to Common Object Request Broker Architecture* (McGraw-Hill).

Newcomer, E. (2002). *Understanding Web Services: XML, WSDL, SOAP, and UDDI* (Addison-Wesley).

Ngu, A. H., Carlson, M. P., Sheng, Q. Z., and Paik, H.-Y. (2010). Semantic-based mashup of composite applications, *IEEE Transactions on Services Computing* **3**, 1, pp. 2–15.

Nierstrasz, O. (1995). Research topics in software composition, in *Proceedings of Languages et Modèles à Objets* (Nancy), pp. 193–204.

Nierstrasz, O. and Dami, L. (1995). Component-oriented software technology, in O. Nierstrasz and D. Tsichritzis (eds.), *Object-Oriented Software Composition* (Prentice-Hall), pp. 3–28.

Nierstrasz, O. and Meijler, T. D. (1995). Research directions in software composition, *ACM Computing Surveys* **27**, 2, pp. 262–264.

Nierstrasz, O. and Tsichritzis, D. (eds.) (1995). *Object-Oriented Software Composition* (Prentice-Hall International).

OASIS (2007). Web services business process execution language, http://docs.oasis-open.org/wsbpel/2.0/OS/wsbpel-v2.0-OS.html.

OMG (2003). UML 2.0 Infrastructure Final Adopted Specification, http://www.omg.org/cgi-bin/apps/doc?ptc/03-09-15.pdf.

OMG (2004). *Common Object Request Broker Architecture: Core Specification, Version 3.0.3*, http://www.omg.org/technology/documents/corba_spec_catalog.htm.

OMG (2005). UML Profile for Schedulability, Performance, and Time, version 1.1, http://www.omg.org/spec/SPTP/1.1/.

OMG (2011). UML Profile for MARTE: Modeling and Analysis of Real-time Embedded Systems, version 1.1, http://www.omg.org/spec/MARTE/1.1.

Oracle (2017). Java web page, http://www.oracle.com/technetwork/java/.

Ossher, H., Kaplan, M., Katz, A., Harrison, W., and Kruskal, V. (1996). Specifying subject-oriented composition, *Theory and Practice of Object Systems* **2**, 3, pp. 179–202.

Ostermann, K. and Mezini, M. (2001). Object-oriented composition untangled, in *Proceedings of Conference on Object-Oriented Programming, Systems, Languages, and Applications* (ACM), pp. 283–299.

Ousterhout, J. (1998). Scripting: Higher-level programming for the 21st century, *Computer* **31**, 3, pp. 23–30.

Pautasso, C. (2009). Composing RESTful services with JOpera, in *Proceedings of International Conference on Software Composition* (Springer), pp. 142–159.

Perry, D. and Wolf, A. (1992). Foundations for the study of software architecture, *ACM Software Engineering Notes* **17**, 4, pp. 40–52.

Pfister, C. and Szyperski, C. (1996). Why objects are not enough, in *Proceedings of 1st International Component Users Conference* (SIGS Publishers).

Platt, D. S. (2003). *Introducing Microsoft .NET*, 3rd edn. (Microsoft Press).

Pohl, K., Böckle, G., and Van Der Linden, F. (2005). *Software Product Line Engineering: Foundations, Principles, and Techniques* (Springer).

Prasanna, D. R. (2009). *Dependency Injection* (Manning Publications Co.).

Prehofer, C. (2002). Feature-oriented programming: A fresh look at objects, in *Proceedings of European Conference on Object Oriented Progtramming* (Springer), pp. 419–443.

Prieto-Diaz, R. (1991). Implementing faceted classification for software reuse, *Communications of the ACM* **34**, 5.

Reussner, R., Becker, S., Burger, E., Happe, J., Hauck, M., Koziolek, A., Koziolek, H., Krogmann, K., and Kuperberg, M. (2011). The Palladio component model, Tech. rep., Karlsruhe Institute of Technology - Faculty of Informatics.

Royce, W. (1970). Managing the development of large software systems: Concepts and techniques, in *Proceedings of IEEE WESCON 26* (IEEE Computer Society), pp. 1–9.

Russell, J. and Cohn, R. (2012). *Microsoft Interface Definition Language* (Book on Demand).

Sametinger, J. (1997). *Software Engineering with Reusable Components* (Springer-Verlag).

SCA-IBM (2017). Service Component Architecture (SCA), http://www.ibm.com/support/knowledgecenter/SSGMCP_5.1.0/com.ibm.cics.ts.application programming.doc/bundleinterface/sca.html.

Schmerl, B. and Garlan, D. (2004). AcmeStudio: Supporting style-centered architecture development, in *Proceedings of International Conference of Software Engineering*, pp. 704–705.

Schneider, J. and Nierstrasz, O. (1999). Components, scripts and glue, in L. Barroca, J. Hall, and P. Hall (eds.), *Software Architectures – Advances and Applications* (Springer-Verlag), pp. 13–25.

Scribner, K., and Stiver, M. C. (2000). *Understanding Soap: Simple Object Access Protocol* (Sams).

Sentilles, S., Vulgarakis, A., Bures, T., Carlson, J., and Crnkovic, I. (2008). A component model for control-intensive distributed embedded systems, in M. R. V. Chaudron,

C. Szyperski, and R. H. Reussner (eds.), *Proceedings of International Symposium on Component-Based Software Engineering, Programming and Software Engineering*, Vol. 5282 (Springer), pp. 310–317.

Shaw, M., DeLine, R., Klein, D. V., Ross, T. L., Young, D. M., and Zelesnik, G. (1995). Abstractions for software architecture and tools to support them, *IEEE Transactions on Software Engineering* **21**, 4, pp. 314–335.

Shaw, M. and Garlan, D. (1996). *Software Architecture: Perspectives on an Emerging Discipline* (Prentice Hall).

Sheng, Q. Z., Qiao, X., Vasilakos, A. V., Szabo, C., Bourne, S., and Xu, X. (2014). Web services composition: A decades overview, *Information Sciences* **280**, pp. 218–238.

Siegel, J. (2000). *CORBA 3 Fundamentals and Programming* (Wiley Computer Publishing).

Sobr, L. and Tuma, P. (2005). SOFAnet: Middleware for software distribution over internet, in *Proceedings of the 2005 International Symposium on Applications and the Internet*, pp. 48–53.

Sommerville, I. (2004a). *Software Engineering*, 7th edn. (Addison Wesley).

Sommerville, I. (2004b). *Software Engineering*, chap. 19: Component-based software engineering, 7th edn. (Addison Wesley), pp. 439–461.

Spillner, A. (2002). The W-Model – strengthening the bond between development and test, in *Proceedings of International Conference on Software Testing, Analysis and Review*.

Szyperski, C. (2002a). Back to universe, *Software Development* (September issue).

Szyperski, C. (2002b). Universe of composition, *Software Development* (August issue).

Szyperski, C., Gruntz, D., and Murer, S. (2002). *Component Software: Beyond Object-Oriented Programming*, 2nd edn. (Addison-Wesley).

Taylor, R. N., Medvidovic, N., and Dashofy, E. M. (2009). *Software Architecture: Foundations, Theory, and Practice* (Wiley Publishing).

van Ommering, R. and Bosch, J. (2002). Components in product-line architecture, in I. Crnkovic and M. Larsson (eds.), *Building Reliable Component-Based Software Systems* (Artech House), pp. 207–221.

van Ommering, R., van der Linden, F., Kramer, J., and Magee, J. (2000). The Koala component model for consumer electronics software, *IEEE Computer* **33**, 3, pp. 78–85.

Velasco Elizondo, P. and Lau, K.-K. (2010). A catalogue of component connectors to support development with reuse, *The Journal of Systems and Software* **83**, pp. 1165–1178.

Vulgarakis, A., Suryadevara, J., Carlson, J., Seceleanu, C., and Pettersson, P. (2009). Formal semantics of the ProCom real-time component model, in *Proceedings of 35th Euromicro Conference on Software Engineering and Advanced Applications* (IEEE), pp. 478–485.

Weerawarana, S., Curbera, F., Duftler, M., Epstein, D., and Kesselman, J. (2001). Bean markup language: A composition language for JavaBeans components, in *Proceedings of the 6th conference on USENIX Conference on Object-Oriented Technologies and Systems* (USENIX Association), pp. 173–188.

WSDL (2001). *Web Services Description Language (WSDL) - Version 1.1*, Ariba, Microsoft and IBM, http://www.w3.org/TR/2001/NOTE-wsdl-2001 0315

Index

Printed in the United States
By Bookmasters